Books that make you better

Books that make you better. That make you *be* better,
do better, *feel* better. Whether you want to upgrade your
personal skills or change your job, whether you want to
improve your managerial style, become a more powerful
communicator, or be stimulated and inspired as you work.

Prentice Hall Business is leading the field with a new breed of
skills, careers and development books. Books that are a cut
above the mainstream – in topic, content and delivery – with
an edge and verve that will make you better, with less effort.

Books that are as sharp and smart as you are.

Prentice Hall Business.
We work harder – so you don't have to.

For more details on products, and to contact us, visit
www.pearsoned.co.uk

instant
entrepreneur

the faster way
to start-up success

Robert Ashton

PEARSON
Prentice Hall
BUSINESS

Harlow, England • London • New York • Boston • San Francisco • Toronto
Sydney • Tokyo • Singapore • Hong Kong • Seoul • Taipei • New Delhi
Cape Town • Madrid • Mexico City • Amsterdam • Munich • Paris • Milan

PEARSON EDUCATION LI

Edinburgh Gate
Harlow CM20 2JE
Tel: +44 (0)1279 623623
Fax: +44 (0)1279 431059
Website: www.pearsoned.co.uk

First published in Great Britain in 2009

© Pearson Education 2009

The right of Robert Ashton to be identified as author of this work has been asserted by him in accordance with the Copyright, Designs and Patents Act 1988.

ISBN: 978-0-273-72061-4

British Library Cataloguing-in-Publication Data
A catalogue record for this book is available from the British Library

Library of Congress Cataloging-in-Publication Data
A catalog record for this book is available from the Library of Congress

10 9 8 7 6 5 4 3 2 1
12 11 10 09 08

Text design by Sue Lamble
Typeset in 9/13.5pt Stone Serif by 30
Printed and bound in Great Britain by Ashford Colour Press Ltd., Gosport

The publisher's policy is to use paper manufactured from sustainable forests.

contents

Managing the business 123

# introduction

Since I first started my own business in 1990 I've made countless mistakes. It was how I learned to be an entrepreneur. Many of those lessons were tough, some were costly and there were plenty of sleepless nights. Of course there were plenty of successes too. But not all were recognised at the time. With hindsight, I'd have spotted and exploited some of those opportunities sooner. But then I didn't have a book like this to help me.

I've not built a multi-million pound empire, nor have I lost money. I've made a very good living and set myself up for a comfortable old age. I've put two children through private education and university. I've always had a nice car, good holidays and no boss to tell me what to do. I am totally debt free and live in a delightful barn conversion surrounded by open fields.

Looking back there are countless decisions I would have made differently. There are things I'd not have done, people I'd not have hired and work I'd have turned away. There were times when I made stupid investment decisions without a proper plan. There were also times when I got it wonderfully right; often by chance! This book will help you succeed faster.

For most of the past 15 years I have worked with business support agencies. I've also owned and run marketing companies, helping other entrepreneurs build their businesses. This book is based as much on what I have observed as on what I have done myself. Everyone makes mistakes in business but I want you to avoid as many as you possibly can. This book will help you to do just that. It can't make you an instant success but it can stop you being an instant failure!

this book will help you succeed faster

In my view, plagiarism is a vastly underrated business process. You simply don't have to re-invent the wheel every time. It's far simpler to learn from decisions others have made and then in time come either to applaud or to regret. Clearly you mustn't rip off intellectual property, patents and the like; that can land you in very hot water. But there's a lot you can learn from others. I hope you find ideas in this book that help you get where you're going quicker, with much less pain and rapid gain.

There is one final point I'd like to make before letting you explore this book further. It's a phenomenon that has puzzled me for years, and only recently have I been able to find proof to support it. That is the fact that people often talk before they can walk. In other words, they make bold claims, promises and offers, long before they have the capacity or experience to deliver. It was one of those online business networking websites that finally brought the truth home to me. People described their business as they wanted it to be, not as it actually is right now.

people often talk before they can walk

It's important to realise that the people who seem to be doing better than you in reality are often doing far worse. Together we will have your business growing quickly, safely and profitably. Your success will be a reality and not an illusion.

Good luck.

preparation

getting ready
shortcuts to preparing yourself

- ☑ What makes a successful entrepreneur?
- ☑ The secrets of objectivity over emotion
- ☑ Why passion can make almost anything possible
- ☑ Have you got what it takes? A simple self assessment

Why set goals?

Entrepreneurs set goals. They work out what they want to achieve then plan how they're going to do it. The more ambitious the entrepreneur, the more ambitious the goals they set themselves.

If you've always been an employee, you'll have had your work goals set for you. When you start a business, you need to set your own.

Goals need to be:

- ☑ achievable, but only just – you want goals that stretch you
- ☑ measurable and broken down into stages so you can chart your progress
- ☑ enjoyable because entrepreneurship should be fun as well as rewarding.

Long-term goals

It helps to have a long-term goal to aim for. The journey may waver and be tough at times, but truly successful people never lose sight of the end goal.

People I know have defined success as:

- buying a country estate and restoring it to its former glory
- not feeling guilty about buying the best seats at the theatre
- starting a charitable foundation
- being able to retire at 50
- creating a business their children can one day take over
- buying a Porsche.

As you can see, it's not really about money. More about what money can make possible. The successful entrepreneur works out how much he or she needs to realise a dream and goes for that.

Short-term goals

set short-term goals that take you closer to your long-term vision

Once you have your sights fixed on the big picture, you have to plan the journey. Set short-term goals that take you closer to your long-term vision. These need to be very specific and easy to measure. Make sure you map out the entire journey. Celebrate each milestone as it is reached; it means you're closer to your long-term goal.

In general, your long-term goal will remain constant. Your short-term goals will evolve and change as you fight your way round the inevitable obstacles to success.

Accepting hard work

It's all too easy to forget that every successful, laid-back entrepreneur you meet once worked hard to generate that success. You're rarely aware today of tomorrow's successful people. Right now they're busy building that success. They keep their heads down and get on with the job. You probably need to do the same.

Sacrifices made in their early days by successful people I know include:

- sleeping in the car on sales trips to save on hotel bills
- being a postman to make a living and working on their business in the afternoons and evenings
- making stuff at night and going out selling it the next day
- persuading the kids to spend their weekend assembling mail shots or dropping leaflets through doors.

Ask any successful entrepreneur about hard work and they'll tell you they've done lots of it. It's a point to remember when all you see is a tough uphill struggle and everyone else seems to be having a good time.

Stepping out from an employer

Malcolm worked his way up from the shopfloor to the boardroom of his company. A change in policy meant that one contract, to source components, assemble, then despatch products for one customer, ceased being viable for his employer. For a new small business, however, it was the perfect opportunity.

Malcolm resigned and, with the consent of his former boss, took over the contract. He rented a factory and used temporary staff to fulfil orders as they came in. Often he worked through the night to save on labour. Now, ten years later he employs 30 people and has time to enjoy his golf!

Knowing yourself

An entrepreneur is someone who sees an opportunity and takes a risk to exploit it. People who are not entrepreneurs are those who come up to you and say, 'I was going to do that,' then go on to explain why circumstances conspired to stop them going ahead.

Successful entrepreneurs are those that:

- have the vision to see what's possible
- know themselves well enough not to take on too much
- are brave enough to take the risk.

Sometimes, like Malcolm, the knowledge that entrepreneurs need to succeed is very well known. All Malcolm did was take what he did at work and do it for himself. Others have seen something work in one place and introduced it somewhere else.

top tip

If you're stuck for inspiration and want to start a business, take a holiday. See how differently people in other countries do a business you understand well. Lots of people find success through introducing a concept to one country that's already been proven in another.

Be objective

We all find ourselves torn at times between our head and our heart. The successful, experienced entrepreneur is as good at saying no as he or she is at saying yes. Years of practice have taught the tough lessons of objectivity. Emotional attachment to a potential project can give you the drive to achieve. It can also cloud your judgement and see you embark on an impossible mission.

the successful entrepreneur is good at saying no

An example of good objectivity

Judith was a social worker. She was also passionate about the way aromatherapy massage could calm the most troubled of minds. Her work brought her into contact with severely disturbed people who were considered too dangerous to live in the wider community.

She practised aromatherapy massage on this client group in the course of her work and saw for herself the positive impact it made.

She recognised that if she could work with disturbed long-term care they would be less challenging and c look after.

Judith allowed her passion and her proven experience into setting up her own business. She helped private sector care homes calculate the value of her work with their residents and charged a fair hourly rate. She soon became very busy.

An example of poor objectivity

Helen had worked in catering all her life. She'd managed works canteens and recently had begun teaching evening classes in food hygiene. She'd always had a boss and was content with her life.

Then her marriage failed. One of her husband's most hurtful jibes had been to accuse Helen of lacking courage and ambition. She'd been happy to have her job and focus on raising the couple's two children.

Shortly after her husband left her she saw that a small, local café she knew had become vacant. She decided to prove to her ex that she had ambition, left her job and signed a three-year lease.

She soon discovered that while she loved cooking for her customers, she found the front-of-house aspect of work difficult. She also took any criticism too personally. Furthermore a new supermarket café was proving to be both convenient and popular. Helen soon ran out of money and hope.

Can you spot the differences between the two examples?

Judith (good example):

- wanted to help people
- knew she could add value
- left work when she was ready
- was destined to succeed.

Helen (poor example):

- wanted to prove a point
- had not done her homework
- left work before she was ready
- was doomed from the start.

How objective are you?

Ask yourself these five questions. If you can honestly answer yes to at least three of them, you're probably being objective. Each question relates to a business opportunity that has caught your eye.

1 If this one doesn't happen, will I keep looking?

2 Will my family be happy to see me doing this?

3 Do my costings still show a profit if my sales fall 20 per cent below my projection and people take 30 days longer than I expect to pay?

4 If after six months someone offers me a lot of money for my new business, will I consider selling?

5 Have at least three people who are not family or friends convinced me that it's such a good idea that they'll become customers?

top tip

Objective entrepreneurs often change their minds. If something you're embarking on looks as if it's not going to work, back out before it's too late. Losing face is painful, losing money can be disastrous!

Why passion matters

Passion is what drives many successful people. It gives them the single-mindedness to really go for it and overcome every obstacle. But however passionate you are about your venture you do need to recognise that some things are simply not possible. That's why this section follows on from a simple 'objectivity test'.

Seasoned entrepreneurs are passionate about their businesses, but also practical. They know the importance of only promising the possible, both to their customers and to themselves.

You can see passion in people who:

- are enthusiastic, convincing and want you to experience what they are promoting
- always have a good answer when you say you're not interested
- create something amazing, seemingly out of thin air
- always seem to be the centre of attention for the right reasons!

Passion gives you huge amounts of self-confidence and makes you single-minded in what you do. I think that passion is best illustrated by religious evangelists. They stand up and publicly promote what they fervently believe in. What's more they carry on regardless, in the face of rejection, ridicule and even physical attack.

If you visit London's Oxford Street there's an evangelist called Tony who spends every day regaling the crowds. Even though people ignore him, shout at him and jostle him he keeps going. His passion and determination have found him public recognition; he's been interviewed on national television several times.

Entrepreneurs who display passion also find themselves in the public eye. Sir Richard Branson is a good example. His constant battling against what he sees as unfair

you cannot learn to be passionate

competition that restricts consumer choice has both won him endless media coverage and made him very wealthy. His battles with British Airways are good examples.

How to find passion

You cannot learn to be passionate – you have to feel it deep inside. Passion happens when you honestly believe that you are right and have what others need (even if they say they don't want it).

It is also possible to build a successful business without passion. You simply do the work and bank the proceeds. However, people who are passionate about their businesses always do better. They are more determined.

Here are some examples of how passionate entrepreneurs describe their enterprises.

- ◢ 'We sell flowers that make people happy' (florist)
- ◢ 'Our phone tariffs let people talk to their friends for longer' (mobile phone company)
- ◢ 'Our organic vegetable boxes contain tasty treats that are good for you too' (organic farmer)
- ◢ 'Flying with us is the most relaxing way to travel' (airline).

The one thing each example has in common is an emotional benefit. These are all people or organisations that believe they can make their customers happier, friendlier, healthier or more relaxed.

People who are not passionate about their business can only see the physical aspects of it. They promise things like 'value for money', 'low cost', 'wide range' or 'high quality'. All of these are important, but given the choice, most buyers will choose something that makes them feel better, rather than simply does the job.

top tip

Everyone is passionate about something. Find what you're passionate about in life. Think about how it affects your enthusiasm and judgement. How can you make your enterprise feel this exciting?

Passion adds real value

Successful entrepreneurs know that passion adds value without adding cost. In other words, if you can give your product or service emotional appeal it appears more valuable to the customer.

A good example of this is Nilfisk. They have a range of commercial vacuum cleaners that are basically tubs on wheels with a lid and a hose. They decided to put a smiling face on the tub and make the lid look like a hat. They gave the products names like Henry. This all helps to humanise the product and make it more emotionally appealing to the customer.

Have you got what it takes? A simple self assessment

Let's be honest. Almost anyone can behave entrepreneurially and find some degree of success. What's important is that you set out to do what you know deep down is right for you. No successful entrepreneur gets to the top by trying to copy someone else. To be successful, you need to lead.

Here are 10 statements for you to consider. Score your answers 1, 2, 3 or 4. Put 1 if you agree totally and 4 if you disagree totally.

1 I am very clear about what I want life to look like
   in three years' time.   _____

2 I've discussed my life goals with my family and
   they agree that I'm being realistic.   _____

3 I've worked out what I want to have in terms of
   income and assets.   _____

4 I can see that what I'm doing right now is
   preparing me for the future I want for myself.   _____

5 I've taken some hard knocks over the years and
   know how to handle stress.   _____

6 I can clearly demonstrate where I have achieved
   a result where others thought I would fail.   _____

7 Hard work doesn't frighten me, I know I have the
   stamina to succeed.   _____

8 My family commitments will allow me the time
   to do what is needed.   _____

preparation
getting ready: shortcuts to preparing yourself

9 I am convinced that I'm not simply running away
from a job I don't enjoy.   _____

10 I promise I'll read the rest of this book!   _____

Total   _____

The lower the total, the greater are your chances of success.

A tale of two entrepreneurs

Once upon a time there were two friends who worked together for a city coach firm. Both were drivers and both enjoyed life behind the wheel. Tom was bright, although he'd not done well at school. He'd never really seen the point. Richard was also bright but more laid-back. He was happy to take life as it came.

Then Harry, who owned the coach company, decided to retire. He had already suggested to Tom and Richard that they buy him out and they broadly agreed. It was a small firm with five coaches and Harry agreed to be paid in instalments. Importantly, Harry also agreed to stay around to help the pair as they got to grips with the business.

The takeover went well, with Tom and Richard jointly owning and managing the business. Things were good for a couple of years and then they started to go wrong.

Tom was ambitious and wanted to grow the business. Richard, on the other hand, was content to keep things as they were. They parted company. Richard took two coaches and a few regular contracts and re-launched as 'Richard's Rovers'. Tom kept the original firm, re-mortgaged his house and went for it.

Today, both men are successful entrepreneurs. Tom has a fleet of 80 coaches and has diversified into HGV maintenance, driver training and continental holidays. His business turns over £4 million per year and is very profitable.

Richard now has five coaches and a loyal local customer base. He tends to work in the office around half the time, spending the rest behind the wheel. He turns over £500,000 per year and earns a good living.

The moral of this tale is simple. You cannot judge the success of an entrepreneur by what he or she achieves in financial terms alone. Both men have profitable businesses. Both have grown their business to the size they feel most comfortable with. Both have the lifestyle and income they want.

If you're going to be a successful entrepreneur you too must work out where you want to be and then get there. It really doesn't matter what other people are doing. Your business, your life and your future are all that matter.

and finally...

Now think about:

- What are your life goals and how can your enterprise deliver them?

- What drives your passion, commitment and enthusiasm for the journey?

- What things are holding you back and how can you change them?

preparation
getting ready: shortcuts to preparing yourself

getting started
shortcuts to successful business ideas

- How to choose and use your business heroes
- Shortcut your way to a good plan
- Quick and effective market research
- Why pioneers often don't get rich

Get a business hero

The best businesses in the world are those that find better ways to do what's already being done. So it makes sense to start by looking at what others have done as you work out your own plans. I like to make those people my heroes and learn from them all that I can.

> heroes are people who might have started where you are now

Heroes are people who might have started where you are now. They've completed the journey you're making. Why not learn from their experience?

Choosing heroes

The more you have in common with your business heroes, the more you can learn from them. They also need to share your values. You want to feel comfortable following their examples.

Heroes can be famous, such as Richard Branson; long dead, for example Alexander Fleming (who discovered penicillin by accident!); or simply someone you've met locally and been impressed by.

Choose heroes that:

- have succeeded in a field you understand
- you can research, hear speak or even meet
- have made a life journey you can relate to.

Using heroes

How you use a hero to shape your thinking and develop your enterprise depends on who that hero is.

Dead heroes:

- you can read their story and learn from what they did
- copy their techniques and challenge convention as they did
- they can also reassure you when you step 'outside the box'.

Famous heroes:

- researching their successes/failures can give you highly relevant tips for today
- you can hear them speak at conferences and get to ask them questions
- providing you don't ask too much of them, you can seek their endorsement/guidance from time to time.

Local heroes:

- will often feel flattered to be approached for advice
- might agree to mentor you as you follow in their footsteps
- often have the potential to make valuable introductions.

My own heroes

It will help you see the potential of heroes if I share with you the identity of two people whose success I am trying to copy.

My first hero is Charles Handy, the management writer. He is around 20 years older than me and we were both first published at a similar age. By looking at his writing career, particularly at how it has evolved, I find I have a benchmark against which to set my own goals and measure my progress. I am fortunate enough to have got to know him over the years and this helps too.

My second hero is Lord (Andrew) Mawson. I first read about Andrew's work in one of Handy's books. Andrew Mawson is a visionary social entrepreneur who established a thriving community project in London's East End. I find many lessons in Andrew's work, particularly the importance of letting others take ownership, rather than trying to change the world all on my own.

top tip

As your enterprise develops and your ambitions evolve, so too must your collection of heroes. Be prepared to outgrow and replace them as you go through your career and your life.

How to find inspiration

The best businesses are those that fill an obvious, but as yet unplugged, market gap. For example, you spot that more people are using bicycles in your town but there's no decent repair shop. Neighbouring towns all have thriving bike repair places and you can see how you can borrow good ideas from two of them to combine in your own business.

Perhaps you've also spotted an empty unit for rent next to the railway station. This means you can service commuters' bikes while they're away, as well as rent bikes to visitors to the town who arrive by train. Lastly, you are an enthusiastic cyclist yourself and enjoy stripping down and fixing bikes.

Because you are a cyclist you see things that others will miss. Equally, others will see opportunities that you miss, but are 'right up their street'. That is how you find the inspiration for your own business.

Five questions to ask yourself

For most of us, the best business ideas are those that seem to drop into our laps. If you're struggling to think of an idea, then you're probably looking in the wrong place. Ask yourself these five questions and see what springs to mind:

1 What do I enjoy doing/am good at that people will value and pay for?

2 How do I want to spend my time?

3 Who do I already know who would become my customers?

4 What can I see that works in other places but isn't being done here?

5 At work, what opportunities can I see that would be great for me but probably wouldn't be economic for my employer to develop?

Sibelius Software

At the age of 10, Ben Finn was a chorister at King's College Cambridge. He later studied music there. He taught himself how to write software and used it to harmonise Bach chorales. He also proof read music for composer Sir Peter Maxwell Davies.

Ben realised that, while word processing was used by authors, composers today still created written manuscripts as they had always done. Together with his twin brother Jonathan he created Sibelius Software and developed what he described to me as 'word processing for music'.

Once the brothers had developed the product they found a ready market. Sibelius grew quickly and won numerous awards. They sold the business in 2006.

The Finns succeeded because:

- *they knew their subject*
- *they could see a clear market opportunity*
- *there was a parallel success to text in word processing.*

Get a ready-made business plan

Banks don't judge a business plan by its weight! The best business plans are those that are short, focused, positive and realistic. You can find plenty of model business plans into which you can conveniently slot your words and figures. Banks offer them, business advice agencies offer them and so too do some of the larger accountancy firms.

However, the trap you can easily fall into is simply to download and fill in one of these weighty documents. It's a trap because the plan blueprint was inevitably prepared to cover all possible business situations and eventualities. Most won't apply to your business and so using these templates commits you to a largely pointless paper chase to fill in all the boxes.

the best business plans are those that are short, focused, positive and realistic

Worse still, the resulting document is not convincing as your vision is drowned in detail. It will also fail to win you favours from even the friendliest bank manager.

How to write your own business plan

Writing your own business plan is simple. It really is, providing you stick to the following two rules.

- Rule 1: write no more than three pages of A4.
- Rule 2: support your proposal with a one-page, simple spreadsheet.

Here are some convenient paragraph headings for you to use. Literally write no more than one, or at the most two, paragraphs about each topic.

Business purpose

What is your business going to improve, change or support?

My business will provide older people with a gardening and DIY service. This will enable more people to live independently for longer.

Why now?

What is the opportunity you've seen that means this should happen now and not later?

People are living longer, many are retiring to this stretch of coast and falling house prices makes downsizing less appealing for the retired.

Your marketplace

How big is your potential market and how is it growing/changing?

There are 18,000 people aged over 60 in the borough, of whom 5,000 are aged over 80. My business will be profitable with 90 customers so I need to convert 0.5 per cent of the target population into regular customers.

Your products and services

What are you going to provide that people will pay for?

The product will be my time. I will agree an annual budget with each customer and then do what needs to be done according to the time of year and what problems have arisen.

The right price

Where will you pitch your price?

I will charge my time at £25 per hour and charge extra for materials and fuel used. I will recruit 90 customers in the first year, who will each buy on average 20 hours of my time. I will be cheaper than a specialist tradesman and more versatile too.

Estimating profit

How much margin do you plan to make and what are the overhead costs that have to be covered before you make real profit for you? How will your sales/profits grow with time?

My first year's budget is:

Sales

£45,000 (90 customers buying 20 hours at £25/hour)

Costs

Travel: £2,000
Phone/postage: £1,000
Advertising/leaflets: £3,000
Tools/clothing: £1,000
Insurance: £1,000
Fees: £500
Contingency: £1,500

Total costs: £10,000

Profit: *£35,000*

Product promotion

How are you going to spread the word and how will you measure your return on marketing expenditure?

Everything we do will make it easy for customers to introduce us to their friends and neighbours. We will use leaflets and incentives to do this, with Yellow Pages advertising providing a 'catch all' back up.

Calculating risks

What are the risks you can see and how will you reduce the chance of them happening?

My health – protected by insurance.

Old people unable to afford me – will switch to younger, busy people.

Litigation – will have full, effective public liability, etc. cover.

As you write remember that:

- you are passionate about this business idea
- your reader only knows what you tell them
- jargon and acronyms are bad
- you should assume that English is your reader's second language, so don't be confusing.

Measuring financial performance

Whilst the narrative element of your plan is to some extent an act of creative writing, the spreadsheet needs to be very accurate. You can't afford to leave anything out by mistake.

top tip

You can download a super free cash flow spreadsheet from the UK Business Advisors website www.ukba.co.uk (they also have a pretty good business plan template too).

Market research – the fast way

There's an old saying that when you start out in business 'you don't know what you don't know'. In other words, it's all too easy to step into a new venture blissfully ignorant of the problems you might encounter.

There are two ways to approach this. You can spend ages researching, planning and worrying about what might or might not be there. Alternatively you can just leap in and hope for the best. It's like swimming in a river. Some people stand on the bank and poke about with a stick to see how deep the water is; others simply jump in and feel for the bottom with their feet. Which would you be?

Market knowledge is very much like a river. You can spend ages trying to measure it, but often it's best to explore it from the inside – even if this means you get wet!

What you already know

When I first wrote a self-help book, I explained to my then editor that I did not feel as confident writing about people as I do about enterprise. Her answer surprised me. She pointed out that as I'd been alive a lot longer than I'd been an entrepreneur, because I had parents, children, a home, friends and interests, I already knew a lot more about life than I gave myself credit for. I bet you're the same.

Most people start a business in an area they know. Otherwise, how could they muster the passion and enthusiasm to take the risk and pitch in? Take time out to cold-bloodedly evaluate your current level of market knowledge. Ask yourself:

- How long have I been involved with the industry I'm in/entering?
- What changes have I seen and what do I predict will change in the future?
- Who do I know that actually knows the territory better than me?

I'm not suggesting you become complacent, more that you stop and take stock of what you already know. You'll be pleasantly surprised!

> **most people start a business in an area they know**

getting started: shortcuts to successful business ideas

preparation

top tip

We are hard-wired to think that everyone else knows what we know, plus a little more. This innate sense of modesty can cloud the reality that, in our own world, we are often world experts.

Where to get free market information

In today's digital age there are very few secrets. Access to the internet and personal pride often combine to leak potentially sensitive market information for your consumption. If you don't believe me, take a look at some blogs published by people in your sector.

There are also myriad organisations that gather and publish data from which you can glean answers to your questions. These include:

- trade associations who use statistics and trends to support lobbying
- government bodies concerned with the labour market and employment
- regional development agencies that publish detailed strategies containing business sector information
- news releases posted on the websites of businesses that supply a sector
- advertising rates of trade publications that often define the market dimensions and the proportion of it their magazines reach
- academics who look at business sectors and abstracts, if not full papers, and can usually be found using a search engine.

top tip

Google Scholar specifically searches academic work. You can sometimes 'discover' inspirational new information here.

Remember as you search that it's as easy to confuse as to inform yourself. So, before you start researching, work out the following:

- How big a market do I need to realise my vision?
- If it's huge, then how will I break it down into segments?
- Which of those segments can I do the best with?

Research the market

Peter retired early from his job in mental health promotion but didn't want to stop working altogether. He knew a lot about stress and how it affects business performance.

He also wanted to travel a bit and so decided to offer his services as a conference speaker. He'd spoken at many sector events and was confident he could both entertain and inform.

He researched his market in two ways. First, he looked at trade organisation conference programmes. He found these quite easily on the internet and built a list of themes and roughly when each organisation held its annual conference. He then searched speaking agencies' websites to see if any offered the same service that he was planning.

He thus had both a list of potential customers and knew exactly what he was competing with. He used all this information to make sure that he offered something different. Not surprisingly Peter soon became a successful conference speaker.

Why being second is often best

Do you remember the Sinclair C5? It was arguably a very good solution to the energy crisis, road overcrowding and global warming. A simple electric vehicle, it had great potential in the eyes of Sir Clive Sinclair, its inventor. However, as a product, it bombed. People found it too different, too unusual and were frightened to set off on a road full of cars protected only by its fibreglass cockpit.

Think now about the G-Whiz. It is also an electric passenger vehicle, small, economical, offering clear benefits to the city dweller over petrol-engined cars. In London, it is exempt from both congestion charge and parking meter fees. It is also not the first of its kind and meets a growing demand. It's more conventional than the C5 and it's easy for the customer to see how it will save them money. If the C5 were invented today it would probably look different and also be more popular with the public. It suffered from being the first of its type.

Being first into a market is a very high-risk strategy. Experienced entrepreneurs like to let other people try new things. They can

it is always safer to start with something that exists and improve it

then pick up the pieces when something new fails and take it to the next stage. It is always safer to start with something that exists and improve it, than to create something totally new.

Even Sibelius Software was not really a totally new concept. It simply took something that worked in one environment (word processing) and applied it in another (preparing music manuscripts).

Safe innovation

Of course innovation is vital. The world needs new things, but there's new and *new*. As you seek to create a new product or service for your enterprise, look for these signs that an opportunity is there for you to exploit.

- New technology means that what was once impossible is now achievable. For example, satellite navigation can make delivery trucks more punctual. How can this translate into customer value/benefit?

- Technology prices are falling so we can now afford to use more advanced systems than before. For example, it's now feasible to use fingerprint recognition as a way of allowing access to buildings. It also enables you for the first time to easily record who's been where, when and for how long. How can this knowledge be used to develop the customer relationship?

- Oil prices are rising fast, which makes fuel economy more of a consumer issue. So more and more companies are looking for alternatives to face-to-face sales calls to customers.

How to keep up to date

It's easy to miss the signs suggesting that an opportunity to try something new exists. You want to let others do the pioneering stuff and then follow up when the time seems right. Good market intelligence therefore is vital.

You can find good market intelligence about new and emerging products and ideas by:

- searching online patent registrations: www.ipo.gov.uk

- reading the right journals

- setting up Google alerts that will email you a link whenever something relevant is posted on the internet: www.google.com.

top tip

The most powerful way to find good market intelligence is Google alerts. Set up the correct search criteria and you will receive links to recently posted information from many sources. Google is so powerful it detects new material that appears even in the most obscure corners of the internet.

and finally...

Now think about:

- Who have you long admired in business and why?

- How are you going to make your business plan really interesting?

- What market information do you need and where are you going to find it easily?

getting funded
shortcuts to raising cash for your business

- Why cash is king in any business
- Quick ways to find funds
- Potential investors you know, but might overlook

Cash is king

Cash is the lifeblood of every business and making sure you have enough, particularly as you grow, is vital. Running out of money is one of the biggest causes of business failure. Here's how the streetwise entrepreneur maximises investment in their business and minimises risk to themselves.

> **running out of money is one of the biggest causes of business failure**

top tip

The novice entrepreneur uses his own money to start a business. The experienced entrepreneur uses as much as possible of someone else's!

Funding your overheads

The amount you need to start your business depends on a number of factors, not least the type of business you're starting. For example, an old folks' home will take a lot more funding than a one-man consultancy business.

Each aspect of a business is funded in a different way, or at least it can be. Here are some examples of what people need money for.

Choosing premises

Most businesses are started at home. Even James Dyson began his business in a shed. Never feel embarrassed about working from home. It's a low-cost, low-risk option and can work surprisingly well. It might not actually cost you anything to work from home.

If you are going to make things, or start that old folks' home, then clearly you need premises. You can buy, rent or lease business premises.

- Buying gives you the opportunity to benefit from any increase in capital values.

- Renting gives you the maximum flexibility if you plan to outgrow premises quickly – you can rent a desk, a room or a building.

- Leasing – buying a lease costs less than buying a building and gives you more security than renting. You can also sell on a lease if you need to move before it has expired.

As with buying a house, your ability to buy commercial premises is usually limited by the amount of money you can put down as a deposit. That's why most business premises are purchased by people with established businesses. When you start, you usually need your spare cash for other things.

top tip

Remember that commercial mortgages are usually arranged over a shorter period than a mortgage on your house. Repayments will therefore be higher.

Buying equipment

It's very easy to get carried away and invest more than you need in plant and equipment. While you do need to make sure you work safely and do not expose customers or employees to undue risk, you can make savings. For example:

- only buy new what you need to buy new
- secondhand can mean more capacity at lower cost
- hire what you only need to use now and again.

top tip

It always costs more to buy equipment on credit than to borrow the money elsewhere and pay a cash price. Equipment credit is almost always at a high interest rate.

Funding those easily forgotten start-up costs

Before you plan how much cash you need to start your business, you need to make sure you include everything you might have to pay for. Your cash flow forecast will show you where to expect peaks of cash demand.

Here are some less obvious costs you might overlook.

- **Marketing**: when you start a business, you are inevitably going to need to invest in promoting it.
- **Recruitment**: if you need staff, you'll have to recruit them. Recruitment agencies are expensive, so is recruitment advertising.
- **Insurance**: public, product, premises and professional liability are some of the things you might want to cover.
- **Loan fees**: you'll be surprised how much you spend on arrangement fees, valuations and the like if you borrow from a bank.

preparation
getting funded: shortcuts to raising cash for your business

Start-up funding fiasco

Andrew worked for a manufacturing business but wanted to work for himself. He resigned, re-mortgaged his house and set up a small factory of his own. He bought all the equipment he'd been used to using at work, which was actually far more than he needed. He had no money left for marketing and, after six unhappy months, his business went bust.

Funding working capital

The smart entrepreneur structures his or her enterprise in a way that minimises the amount of working capital needed. The previous chapter gave you some tips on producing your cash flow forecast and where to find a spreadsheet to download.

Working capital is the money you're going to need to pay your bills while waiting for your customers to pay you. It is the money that remains within a business and that you can rarely touch. It is often money you have to borrow, so minimising the need for it is actually better than finding clever ways to borrow it. Here are some factors that will reduce your need for working capital.

- **Take deposits:** it is only convention that says we do the work, send an invoice and then wait at least a month for the money. Taking a deposit commits the customer and gives you money to buy materials. It also encourages the customer to make sure the job gets finished as they've already part-paid. Build in taking deposits to both your business plan and your business process.

- **Credit cards:** people are quick to complain about the fact that the credit card company takes at least 2.5 per cent of the transaction value, but you do get the money straight away. It's often better for you than having to wait for an invoice to get paid many weeks later.

- **Online:** people expect to pay for things they buy online when they order them. This gives you positive cash flow (you've got payment before you've paid for the goods yourself).

- **Supplier credit:** if you're a new business, your suppliers will appreciate your need to give yourself plenty of cash flow 'headroom'. Negotiate extended credit, say three months, with your main suppliers, pay them punctually and your work capital demand drops.

Finding working capital

Clearly you are going to need some working capital. You can't squeeze it all from cash flow. To calculate how much you need you have to look at your cash flow forecast. Be realistic about how much you're going to need and don't kid yourself by making unrealistic assumptions. Your working capital demand will increase when:

- people pay you later than you anticipated
- jobs take longer to finish than you expected
- you get large bills (particularly unplanned repair bills)
- your business becomes a victim of crime/storm damage, etc.
- your costs rise
- mistakes mean you have to do something again without payment.

Once you have calculated a realistic figure for working capital, you need to obtain it. Ideally you need to find the money to fund your month-to-month cash flow, then negotiate an overdraft facility so that you can borrow when you need more. Places to look for working capital include:

> you are going to need some working capital

- your savings/investments
- family and friends
- re-mortgaging your home
- the lump sum payment from your pension if you're old enough.

If re-mortgaging the family home feels like a bad idea, revisit the business plan. Almost all borrowing has to be guaranteed and that means your home is inevitably at risk if it is the only asset you have.

If you are still stumped for a source of working capital, you could consider the Small Firms Loan Guarantee Fund. Most high street banks can access this government scheme. It enables you to borrow money where you have no assets to offer as security. The risk is effectively insured by an up-front percentage of the loan. There are also significant arrangement fees.

Finding outside investors

Hermann Hauser is a well-known Cambridge-based entrepreneur and venture capitalist. He founded Acorn computers. Some time ago he gave me a valuable piece of business advice. When looking for investors in a young business, he said you should look first for 'family and fools'.

In other words, you usually need to approach people who will invest for emotional rather than logical reasons. It is fair to say that few people would be callous enough to borrow money from their relatives if they thought it would be at risk. However, it is also fair to say that many family feuds have erupted as the result of a naïve entrepreneur losing auntie's life savings!

> approach people who will invest for emotional rather than logical reasons

Here are some good people to invite to invest in your business, with ideas about what each might find appealing.

Family

Your family will invest because it's you. Respect that emotion is clouding their judgement and only take the money if you're sure that (a) you'll be able to pay it back and (b) they can afford to lend it. Consider protecting them by putting in place:

- a proper legal agreement that defines the terms of the loan
- a debenture if they want added protection. (A debenture is a legal charge over your debtor list. It means that if the business fails, the debenture holder gets paid first.)

Friends

Rather like your family, friends must not feel pressured. However, if you have a wide circle of friends, why not encourage them all to lend you a little each? That way, they'll all take an interest in your venture and that has to be good news!

top tip

Warning! Sometimes it can seem like a good idea to involve your friends and family in the business. Only do this if they have relevant skills and experience and there is a clearly defined role for them.

Suppliers

Your suppliers can be a good source of working capital. In addition to offering you extended credit, suppliers can sometimes be encouraged to:

- give you old but serviceable stock at a lower cost
- introduce you to other, non-competing, suppliers, reducing your costs
- pass on customer enquiries, boosting your sales
- give a credit reference to new suppliers, making it easier for you to open accounts.

Customers

Surprisingly, customers can also be a good source of funding for your business. There are several reasons why a customer might do this:

- they want a wider choice of suppliers and want to help you get into the game

- they've had a bumper year and want to pre-pay for future supplies to reduce their tax liability
- the business owner can remember starting out and simply wants to help – yes, this really does happen!

top tip

In the public sector, budgets are often clawed back if not spent before the end of March. This means that some public sector organisations are happy to accept invoices in January and February for yet to be completed work. If you have public sector clients, find out if you can help them spend their budgets in time!

How to deal with banks

Despite what people may tell you, banks *are* on your side. They only want to lend you money if convinced you'll be able to pay it back comfortably. Why would you want to borrow what you can't pay back? Look on your pitch to your bank as free consultancy and heed the advice they give. Even if you disagree with them, recognise that others might see your business in the same way.

Choosing a bank

You already have a relationship with a bank, perhaps with two. However, when you are looking to start or grow a business, you need to take a fresh look at your choice of bank.

The experienced entrepreneur knows that banks:

- have different policies regarding what they will lend on
- have lending targets to hit
- can vary from branch to branch.

There's nothing wrong with inviting a number of banks to consider your proposition. What one rejects, another might accept. Furthermore, the bank you use for your personal affairs might not be the best bet for your business.

top tip

Many entrepreneurs prefer to keep their business and personal banking separate. This prevents your business bank manager knowing what's happening on your personal account.

There are a number of different types of bank.

Internet banks

Some banks are geared specifically to provide an effective online service. You pay low charges (if any) but don't have easy access to a manager. They are ideal for simple businesses that stay in credit, have few transactions and have no need for borrowing.

High street banks

The major banks compete fiercely for the small business market. With 400,000 start-ups a year in the UK it's a big market to go for. They all offer similar services, with both online and face-to-face services. Look at several before choosing one.

Boutique banks

If you're successful, relatively well off and want to enjoy a more bespoke service, try a boutique bank. These are different from the various 'premier' banking services offered on the high street. Their managers have local discretion to make lending decisions and are great if you want to find a simple way of doing complicated things. They don't take on everyone though!

Specialist banks

If you're running a social enterprise, or perhaps would prefer banking that is Sharia'a compliant, you need a specialist bank. Most high street banks can accommodate these and other special needs, but you might find a specialist bank more understanding.

What banks want

Bank managers are no different from anyone else. They want to be respected, to feel they're making a difference and to have a hassle-free life. You can deliver this in return for their support if you:

- are realistic in what you want to achieve with the money they lend

- understand that while they earn interest, you hopefully will make a lot more from the investment

- keep your business plan and any proposals short, simple and sensible

- do not get emotional when they question your motives/plans

- ask 'why?' when they say no and consider adapting your plan before you try another bank.

Boutique bank to the rescue

Christian and his civil partner Ben built up their art gallery over the years and gained a national reputation. They'd always rented their premises and decided that they'd like to convert a riverside warehouse in the city centre. Their vision was to create a contemporary gallery and coffee shop, with a loft apartment for themselves on the top floor. Their business also needed more working capital as they liked to buy some works to sell, as well as simply displaying on a sale-or-return basis.

For a number of reasons, not all of them clear, two high street banks found it too difficult to combine business and personal borrowing for their development. Then they called a Scandinavian boutique bank that had recently opened a branch in their city. The manager seemed to understand their vision for the project and offered some useful advice about how best to structure their business to get the most out of the move. They got their funding and asked their bank manager to cut the ribbon and open the new gallery when the work was finished.

and finally...

Now think about:

- How much money do you need right now in your business?

- Who do you already know that could help in some way?

- Are you using the right bank, or would you be better understood elsewhere?

building the
business

being different
shortcuts to brand and image

- ◢ How to be more visible
- ◢ What your brand says about your business
- ◢ Choosing your key messages

Why brand is important

The better your brand and business image, the less you will need to invest in marketing it. In other words, the smart entrepreneur chooses to present an image that will excite the customer. The novice, however, chooses to present an image that excites them.

This is understandable, if expensive, for the new entrepreneur. If it's the first enterprise, it is very exciting and usually very personal. A first business is like a first kiss, first job, first baby, etc. Although you never lose the passion for enterprise, you do become more objective with the passage of time.

Brand and the small firm

If you operate as a one- or maybe two-man band, you are the business and the brand. You have to look the part because, quite literally, you are the business. In fact as a business grows, those early branding statements need to be adopted by everyone.

You only have to think of Sir Richard Branson to see what I mean. He is instantly recognisable with long hair, beard and colourful jumper. His business values are pretty clear too. He challenges the grey suited corporate world and champions fair play and lower consumer prices. He looks the part.

you have to look the part

In the small organisation, the owner's personal image and brand need to reflect the business they're in. Here are a couple of examples.

How you look

The clothes we wear and the way we style our hair evolves as our interests develop. Our default style of dress is an amalgam of our upbringing and the company we keep. The art of getting the right look is to move to the edge of the stereotype people in your type of business almost inevitably currently conform to. In other words:

- be different, but not extreme
- be consistent and don't stray too far from your chosen style
- adapt as your business evolves.

top tip

Big firms use branding consultancies to develop a logo and house style. If you are the face of your business, use an image consultant instead.

What you say

One of the best ways to be noticeably and memorably different is always to be positive. I'm not suggesting you become sickeningly positive in everything you say and seek out the silver lining to every dark cloud. But remember that most people's response to the question 'how are you today?' is to say 'not too bad'. 'Not too bad' is rather negative when you think about it. Why not say something more positive and always use the same phrase. You could try something like 'outstanding', 'brilliant, thanks' or 'pretty good' instead. You'll soon get known for it and people will respond well to your positive manner.

As well as sounding positive, you want to be known as someone who actively listens. People like to talk about themselves and you will be thought of more highly if you are a good listener, able to nod, focus and direct

you will be thought of more highly if you are a good listener

the flow of conversation so that those you're with can have their say. There's nothing more boring than someone who talks about themselves and their business all the time.

Brand and the larger business

A business becomes more valuable when it has an identity separate from its founder. It's easier to sell a business when it can be clearly seen to be separate from the person selling it. In general, the more you supply services rather than products, the greater the risk of being considered indispensable.

Your business name

You want your business to stand out from its competitors and for prospective customers to immediately see what the business does. Naming your business after yourself, a favourite place or your children might seem like a good idea. Saying what the business does is actually better.

Splashdown

Jayn-Lee Miller started Splashdown after giving birth to her son in a birthing pool. She wanted to make it easier for more women to experience a water birth. She now sells and hires birthing pools all over the UK and is very successful.

A key element of her success is the name of her business – Splashdown. It is memorable, humorous and paints an image in your mind of a baby literally splashing down as it arrives in the world.

When naming a business:

- choose something that says what you do
- try to embed humour or a benefit (such as Fast Cars for taxi hire)
- try not to choose a name that might look silly if you diversify.

His Master's Voice

His Master's Voice was one of the leading brands of gramophone records (and gramophones) in the UK. The famous logo, with Nipper the dog listening to a record being played, was to be seen everywhere.

Today the brand is best known as a recorded music retailer. You can find an HMV store on hundreds of high streets across the nation. Abbreviating the company name enabled the company to modernise and retain its original name.

How others see you

HMV also modernised its image, moving from a dated picture of a dog and gramophone to trendy typography. Business image goes far beyond the logo though. Some very practical ways to make sure your business projects a positive image include:

- having a strong, professionally designed, simple logo
- using good signage, outside and inside your company
- using delivery vehicles that are clean and not dented
- having uniformed employees
- training staff to be able to answer customer questions.

business image goes far beyond the logo

It's fair to say that making the effort to get the detail right can be hard work. You are in your business every day and won't notice if things slip. Visitors, however, will immediately spot if the image is not quite right.

Signs to look for that a business is no longer on the ball include:

- signs with letters missing

- light bulbs not changed when they fail

- scruffy staff

- scuffed décor

- chipped coffee mugs.

Yes, these are all small things, but they are also clear signs that standards are slipping.

top tip

The experienced entrepreneur makes a point of noticing things that need fixing. You need to spot them too.

Products and services that sell themselves

There is no such thing as a unique product or service. If there was, people would be reluctant to buy because there'd be nothing to compare it with.

People make decisions by comparing what's on offer with what they already know about. Successful entrepreneurs develop product/service brands that are easy for their marketplace to compare with something else. Innovative, new products inevitably replace something, making comparison easier.

Examples

- *Eurostar advertising compares the journey time from central London to central Paris with that of airlines. The train travels more slowly but you still get to your destination sooner. It is a railway that presents itself like an airline.*

- *The London transport pre-pay smart card is called Oyster. Initially it's hard to see the connection, but when you think about it, it's actually a valuable electronic chip (the pearl) hidden inside a card, which itself sits in a plastic wallet that opens rather like an oyster shell. Because there was no generic name for this kind of smart card, Oyster (the service name) soon became a generic term in everyday use.*

building the business
being different: shortcuts to brand and image

4

Both of these examples illustrate how large organisations have used comparative branding to highlight customer benefits. Eurostar is faster than flying and Oyster is as desirable as a pearl. Your business is probably smaller, but you need to use the same principles if you're to make it easy for your marketplace to see the benefits you're offering.

When it comes to naming your product or service, here are some points to remember.

Bad product/service names:

- use numbers/letters, such as xyz 365R

- are hard to say

- are unlinked to their function.

Good product/service names:

- use words, such as xyz daily

- are easy to remember

- are specific (say what they do).

top tip

Use homophones wherever you can. These are words that sound the same but have different meanings. For example, a chandler might have a sail sale, or a fish and chip shop might be called the 'Plaice Place'.

Features and benefits

You can see, I hope, that when making comparisons between your product or service and those of others, benefits are more important than features. Benefits are what it *does*; features are what it *is*.

Once you realise that people buy what things do, rather than what they are, your marketing messages become much clearer. Clearer marketing is more effective and so what you're selling becomes more appealing and more likely to 'sell itself'.

Here are some examples of the features and benefits of selected products and services:

Product/service	Feature	Benefit
Pension plan	Good investment record	A dream retirement
Stainless steel hinges	Do not rust	Last longer
Chiropodist	Cared-for feet	Comfortable walking
Camera	Takes photographs	Memories

Benefits of better locks

Declan is a locksmith working in a large city. Until last year, most of his work was replacing locks after break-ins. Luckily the city's burglars kept him fairly busy and he was on a list of locksmiths used by the police. But he wanted to take more control of his business and be more proactive.

He launched a free 'lock-check' service for householders worried about break-ins. People seeking peace of mind would invite him round to check over their homes. He would invite the homeowner to lock their front door and stand with him on the doorstep with a stopwatch. He then picked their lock and was usually inside in less than a minute.

Not surprisingly, many people then took him up on the offer of a replacement lock. He carried a stock of them in his van so was able to fit one there and then. Word soon spread and he became very, very busy.

building the business
being different: shortcuts to brand and image

Brand and reputation

For many of us, small is beautiful. Being a big fish in a small pond can feel a lot more comfortable than being a small fish in a big one. Of course big ponds give you room to grow. But they can contain predators as well!

The inexperienced entrepreneur locksmith may display his locks and bemoan the fact that he is constantly undercut by the DIY sheds.

Declan the locksmith became a specialist, albeit unwittingly. His aim was to become proactive, but his trick of picking the customer's lock, then replacing it is what made him different. (It also proved to be a very fast way to secure a sale.)

Being known for one particular aspect of your business is good. Your reputation as a specialist enhances your brand. It can make marketing easier.

How to become well known

Here are five steps to building your reputation in a particular niche. It doesn't matter if you've been trading for years or have just started. You might work on your own or employ 100, it doesn't matter. The principles are the same.

1 Work out exactly what you do best, enjoy the most and face least price competition delivering. Pick the single activity where you almost always win the business and make money too.

2 Think about what this aspect of your work really is. It could be that you sell products but the service is most highly valued. What is the 'golden nugget' within that activity that people treasure most?

3 Imagine that this activity is all that your business now does. How will you describe it, brand it, promote it, do it? Only include around it the things that are vital, although in reality less important.

4 Check out your thoughts and ideas with some of the customers who gave you business of this kind. See how they describe what you provided. Also, check out your proposed re-focused offer with some prospective customers.

5 Adapt your marketing/presentation to focus on what you've now recognised as being at the heart of your business opportunity.

Recognising desire lines

What the above exercise may well illustrate is that the elements of your customer offer that you most value might not be those your customers most value. Sometimes, that realisation can be hard to accept. You may even feel affronted that your customers could be so obtuse!

What you are dealing with here are behavioural desire lines. Desire lines are fascinating once you realise what they are. Imagine a public library with an impressive lawn between the building and the road. Concrete paths go up both sides of the lawn and join a path that runs along the front of the building. There's a low wall along the roadside, with gates at the end of each path. Across the centre of the lawn is a well trodden track where people have stepped over the path and taken a short cut to the library door. That is a desire line.

In every aspect of business life, as in life in general, people will create and follow desire lines. Whatever you plan for them, they will inevitably go their own way if it differs from what you've presented.

top tip

A specialist firm is one that recognises a desire line and builds everything around it. The desire line is the most appealing option by default. You need to be there, not necessarily where you started.

and finally...

Now think about:

◢ How would your customers describe you today?

◢ How does your brand image compare with your rivals?

◢ Are you a generalist or a specialist?

getting customers

shortcuts to marketing success

* ▨ Why marketing matters
* ▨ How to promote your business
* ▨ Selling made simple

Why do we need to market?

A business without customers is like a skydiver without a parachute. Both can look impressive for a short while, but without the sales to support you, you soon come down to earth with a sickening thud.

It's easy for the novice to get so wrapped up in creating the business that they delay selling until it's almost too late. Then, they'll clutch at any straw that offers salvation. Advertising is the lifebelt they usually get thrown first. However, it rarely delivers the results they are hoping for.

The seasoned entrepreneur knows that:

* ▨ without customers your business is simply a hobby
* ▨ customers do not always want what you think they need
* ▨ what people will pay and what things cost are largely unrelated.

Affordable publicity

You can't start promoting a business or new activity soon enough.

> you can't start promoting a business or new activity soon enough

The cautious new entrepreneur often believes that you need to keep your idea secret until you really are ready to deliver. The fears are understandable. You don't want to stimulate interest you cannot satisfy; nor do you want to give competitors the chance to learn what you are doing.

Let's shatter two myths:

Myth 1: *You mustn't promote yourself until everything's ready.*

In reality, you need customers as soon as you've had the idea. This is because customers:

- usually enjoy feeling part of your development team
- can help you make the customer offer more appealing
- might fund some of your development work
- mean your new venture hits the ground running.

Myth 2: *Competitors are watching your every move.*

The paranoid amongst you will be disappointed to learn that competitors are usually too busy doing business themselves to worry unduly about you. Unless you're infringing protected intellectual property, they are unlikely to be watching your every move. In fact competitors are good because they:

- help you differentiate your offer
- stimulate market demand that you can also satisfy
- are potential buyers for your business if it succeeds.

So how do you promote your business before you can really afford to?

Word of mouth

The savvy entrepreneur never underestimates the power of word of mouth. People talk, so why not encourage them to talk about you? In fact spreading the word about your new idea, activity or project is free so it makes sense to do it indiscriminately. You simply never know who the people you tell will talk to. Even your hairdresser has the potential to recommend you to someone else whose hair they cut.

never underestimate the power of word of mouth

When talking about your business:

- be positive about what you do and how your customers (will) benefit
- be enthusiastic about the difference your business makes to others
- never knock your competition, however bad they are!

Editorial coverage

If what you are doing is really exciting it is also newsworthy. Newspapers, trade publications, specialist magazines, radio and even television might give you coverage.

You can hire freelance public relations (PR) specialists to write news releases, then distribute them on your behalf. However, it can be just as effective simply to pick up the phone and ring the journalists your research tells you are most likely to write about you.

You have a news story when:

- you are doing something that is significantly new
- what you are doing will make a good photograph
- your story offers a solution to a well publicised problem
- someone famous is endorsing your work.

building the business
getting customers: shortcuts to marketing success

Ignore magazines that say they'll publish your editorial if you pay for an ad or for a picture to be included. These titles are rarely respected by their readers.

Advertising in a nutshell

When you can afford to advertise, do:

- advertise little and often
- tempt readers to visit your website
- use few words and make them work
- make reader response easy.

Don't:

- run just one big ad
- tell the whole story in the ad
- squeeze in lots of text
- forget to add your contact details.

Fast customer targeting

Don't waste time marketing to the wrong people. Narrow down your search by focusing on the people with the greatest potential. For example, driving schools want to sell to parents of 17-year-olds.

don't waste time marketing to the wrong people

Taking the example of the driving school further, they could simply advertise in the local paper and have a Yellow Pages ad. Or they could:

- check the Electoral Register to identify those families with a 17-year-old
- offer 'pre-driving' experiences to secondary schools
- offer an incentive for their pupils to introduce their friends
- sponsor a local 'young driver' competition to raise their profile.

How to target your perfect customers

First, identify your perfect customers. These give you consistent profit and no hassle. What do these people:

- buy from you and what's the value to them?
- have in common with one another?
- tell you are their reasons for buying from you?

Second, work out how many of them you need; in other words convert your sales target into a customer target.

- How much do they spend with me each year?
- How long do they remain customers?
- How many do I need to replace/gain this year?

Third, where can you find them? In particular where do they go or what do they do that people who won't become your customers don't do?

- What do they read? Where do they go?
- What business/lifestyle traits make them different?
- In what towns do they live (preferably you want customers close by)?

Fourth, how can you reach them and people like them? The more specific the medium you use to reach your target group, the cheaper it will be. For example:

- wealthy people read more theatre programmes than free newspapers
- more shoppers will see ads inside park and ride buses than will see them on a roadside hoarding
- mobile home residents are big buyers of garden gnomes. Direct mailing gnome offers to residential parks is actually possible!

Finally, how can you measure your campaign? It's vital once you've found a potentially rich source of the right kind of prospect that you test it. You can test a target niche by:

- mailing them an exclusive offer and seeing what comes back
- advertising with a specific email address for enquiries
- offering the chance to win something in return for completing a simple online survey.

top tip

It's easy to put together a professional online survey. There are websites such as www.surveymonkey.com that make it easy to do. These sites are inexpensive to use; sometimes they're even free.

Targeting higher-value customers

Jason works for himself as a car valeter. Most of his work comes from second-hand car dealers. They give him regular work but at a knock-down price. He also has some private clients; these pay more for a regular monthly valet. They tend to be business people who have nice cars and want to create a good first impression when visiting customers.

To get more high-value private clients, Jason had some postcards printed. On one side were before and after pictures of clients' cars and on the other, a couple of testimonials and an introductory offer. He kept these in his van and, when passing conference centres and business premises, popped them on the windscreens of all the quality cars.

He found that one in twenty prospects rang him up for the offer (a half-price valet). Of these, half remained customers for at least six months. Soon he was able to drop the trade customers for others who paid much more.

Brochures and leaflets – getting them right first time

There's little that massages the ego more than seeing your product or service depicted in a glossy brochure. What's more, people like to collect and compare brochures before making their purchase.

But how does the streetwise entrepreneur avoid spending a fortune on promotional print?

Here are three questions to ask yourself before you start spending:

1   Who is going to request or read the brochure?
2   How am I going to get them into that person's hand?
3   What do I want them to do when they've read it?

Brochures are good:

- when the customer is unlikely to buy at your first meeting and needs a reminder of what your offer is
- in situations where people seek information before they buy
- when they contain dimensions, capacities, colours and other statistics the customer needs to specify their purchase.

Brochures are bad when:

- customers take a brochure as an excuse for not making a purchase
- salespeople give them out instead of engaging the prospect in conversation
- you forget to record who has one and/or don't follow up.

What all promotional print should include

Print is different from advertising. Ads have to grab attention and provoke an enquiry. Print has to inform, reassure and confirm that it was right to enquire and that a purchase is a sensible next step. Here are some useful pointers for when you are preparing leaflets and brochures.

Pictures

If you only invest in one thing, make it professional photography. Good photography makes good print. Photographs should illustrate the benefits of your product/service where possible.

Words

Words should be explicit, simple and jargon-free. Write as if you are speaking to the reader; for instance, 'I think you'll find this works best.'

Size

This depends on your audience. Business-to-business should be A4 so it can be filed and found again. Consumers often prefer things they can slip in their pocket or bag, such as one-third A4. In the UK, A5 is cheaper to post than A4 and can be a useful halfway house between the two extremes.

Format

Promotional print is in many ways a surrogate salesperson and needs to take the reader through a logical sales sequence. Therefore:

- the front cover needs to say/show exactly what you're selling

- the inside needs to explain why it's important, what it does and how it works – compare with alternatives if possible

- the back cover needs to reassure (quality, value statements, etc.) and tell the reader how you can be contacted.

Testimonials

These are good to include where you can. Remember that you will need to ask customers for a testimonial and perhaps help them write it. Successful people solicit testimonials all the time.

top tip

Include urgency – not in the print as this will date it and limit its useful life. Instead, include an incentive to buy before a certain date in the covering letter you send with your printed material.

Where to obtain promotional print

You can buy brochures and leaflets from:

- printers, who can usually design them for you as well

- marketing agencies, who will help you integrate your print in a wider campaign

- online printers, who offer limited choice but bargain basement prices.

Choose the option that best meets your customers' expectations; don't try to save money if it jeopardises your credibility. Cheap print usually looks like cheap print.

Mouse-mat marketing

Hugo has a business that sells office stationery and supplies. He used to pay to have his wholesaler's catalogue overprinted with his details and post them to his customers and prospects. Then he decided to try something different. He ran a monthly competition among stationery buyers (usually office managers) to send him photos of their pets. The winner got a prize and everyone on his list received a mouse-mat bearing the winning photo, his company details and that month's special offer.

Buyers liked the mats and nearly all used them. Whenever anyone needed any office supplies, his company's phone number fell easily to hand. He both saved money and increased his sales.

Quick ways to get recommended by your customers

There are very few businesses that cannot benefit from customer referrals. When a customer recommends you to someone, you can be confident that:

- the referring customer is a satisfied customer

- you're meeting someone new, who's genuinely interested

- the new customer is able to pay and probably knows what you cost

- you need to reassure, not hard sell, to get the business.

If every customer you ever have introduces you to one more customer, you might never need to invest in advertising and promotion.

How to get referrals

The way to encourage your customers to recommend you to their friends, family and contacts is simple. All you have to do is ask. Here are some examples of how you can pop the question.

- *'You're clearly happy with the job we've done. Who else do you know that might also find our work valuable?'*

- *'Most of our work comes from customer recommendation. Who are the two people you know most likely to be interested in what we do?'*

- *'I prefer to invest in my customers rather than in advertising. If you can introduce me to people who become customers, I can give you a £50 voucher as an introduction fee.'*

When to ask

There is a school of thought that says you should let some time elapse before going back to ask for recommendations. But I believe the best time to ask for a recommendation is when the decision to buy is freshly made. Time can only erode recollection of the reasons why buying from you was a good idea.

Embedding referral into your business process

Although this might sound complicated, that is not the case at all.

True entrepreneurs keep things simple and don't 'do' complicated.

In time you will come to realise that there are many ways to encourage people to recommend you to others. But rather than wait to stumble over them, here are some popular examples.

Enquiry form

If your prospective customers give you their details when they request brochures, demonstrations, etc., why not add the following question to the form: 'Please give us the name and contact details of anyone else you think might also be interested in this.' People can complete it or ignore it – give them the choice.

Satisfaction survey

Either a postal or online survey can be sent to your customers to measure their satisfaction. Short, specific, simple surveys show your customer that you care and want to listen to their feedback. They also present opportunities to ask for introductions.

'Bring a friend' offers

Gyms, restaurants, tourist attractions and many other kinds of business can make these offers. You give the customer a voucher as they leave that entitles them to a 'two for one' offer if they return within a certain time and bring a friend. To redeem the voucher they have to give the friend's details. You can then follow up and mail them with incentives to return.

Sample packs

If you run a mail order business, why not include with each consignment a card that, if returned, entitles a friend to a free sample pack? That can itself be followed up with an incentive to purchase.

top tip

Work out what it costs you to recruit new customers via conventional marketing. Invest the same amount per customer in winning referrals. Your costs won't rise, but your sales will.

building the business
getting customers: shortcuts to marketing success

5

Avoid cold calling – get straight to the people who'll say yes

Cold calling, either by phone or letter, is fast becoming unpopular. People don't like being cold called and salespeople hate doing it. Why give yourself the torment when there is a better way to get through to new customers?

> **cold calling is fast becoming unpopular**

Stalking

Yes, the word 'stalking' has some unfortunate connotations, but it is also the correct term to describe the process of 'going through (an area) in search of prey'. It's the way hunters catch big game and the way a cat catches a mouse.

Sales stalking is perhaps a better way to describe it. It is the opposite to opening your shop door and waiting to see who comes in. It's the best way to find new customers when you have a very specific or exclusive product or service.

- *Headhunters use stalking to identify, approach and poach people not actually looking for a new job.*
- *Academics use stalking to find peers in other parts of the world with whom they share a research topic.*
- *Investors use stalking to identify businesses they can offer to buy to plug a gap in their portfolio.*

I use stalking all the time when I want to find someone able to help me with a specific project I might be working on. For example, I was recently asked to help a sheltered workshop that makes wire 'point of sale' products to find new customers. Having decided that charity shops would be particularly receptive to buying from a social enterprise, I set out to build a list of people who managed groups of charity shops. Each was then approached, as an individual. This made the invitation to buy personal and was very successful.

Here is a step-by-step guide for how to stalk:

1 **Work out what you're looking for** and why.

2 **Identify the organisations** most likely to fit your need.

3 **Identify the job roles** and **individuals** most likely to be able to make (or at least influence) the buying decision.

4 **Find out about those individuals** – what is their email address, what is their background, what are their values and interests?

5 **Tailor your approach.** You can now put together a short, personal approach. It could be by email or post. Email allows you to add links to your website. Post enables you to send samples.

6 **Make your approach** – and then follow up quickly. Offer alternatives that might include: meet now, meet later, keep informed of developments, don't contact again.

To gather the information you need sometimes takes painstaking research. This often involves using the internet. As well as using Google or other search engines, check out:

- news archives that may contain articles about your target people

- www.ipo.gov.uk – a UK resource that enables you to find out who owns trademarks and what patents have been recently filed

- financial databases – often accessible for free in public libraries and can give detailed company/director information

- blogs – increasingly being used to express unofficial views and comments about organisations. They can be quite revealing.

top tip

University library websites often have very useful download-able guides to internet search techniques. Check some out and become better at finding exactly what you're looking for.

The three golden rules of stalking

1 **Aim high** – always pursue people who offer the most potential.

2 **Be specific** – busy people want to hear the punchline first. Don't dither.

3 **Don't annoy** – always explain how you came to find them and what assumptions you have made. If they're not interested, don't pester.

Remember that stalking is a very direct form of marketing. Do it well and you will become very successful. Do it badly and you can quickly annoy people.

and finally...

Now think about:

◢ Who are the people most likely to become your next customers?

◢ Where can you find them?

◢ What will influence them enough to give you a call?

getting sales
shortcuts to closing deals

☑ Features and benefits

☑ Asking the right questions at the right time

☑ Making sure your customer knows what they've said yes to

Make selling simple

Selling should be very simple. Nobody likes feeling pressured and nine times out of ten, an order is placed because the decision feels right to both parties. All you have to do is help your prospect see how spending money with you solves a problem.

> the fast way to sell successfully is to keep it simple

The fast way to sell successfully is to keep it simple.

Features and benefits

Understanding the difference between features and benefits is the quickest way to accelerate your sales success. We touched on this topic in Chapter 4 and now we are going to go a bit deeper.

Features

These are what products or services actually are or have. Features are the aspects of your offer that you've sweated to produce. For example:

- a hybrid car has both petrol and electric motors
- a garden centre stocks both bare root and pot grown trees
- a contract cleaning company has a large workforce.

Benefits

These are what products or services do for the customer. Benefits are the aspects of your offer that the customer values most. For example:

- a hybrid car is economical and exempt from London's congestion charge
- stocking both bare root and pot grown trees means customers can buy and plant all year round
- access to lots of cleaners means you're never let down; there's always someone to come and do the job.

How to use features and benefits

Good salespeople are those who effectively translate relevant features into relevant benefits. They ask questions to find out what challenges their customer and then describe how their product or service overcomes that challenge. Equally, customers are rarely interested in features they can see no application for.

benefits are the aspects of your offer that the customer values most

Imagine for a moment that you sell wheelbarrows. You stock a range of premium priced, high specification barrows. Key features include:

- twin wheels which make them more stable
- galvanised body which means they don't rust
- puncture resistant tyres.

Then some customers come in to buy a barrow. They've seen a cheaper one elsewhere, but just want to check out your product before buying. You have to persuade them that your barrow is worth the premium.

The poor salesperson lists all the features and hopes the customer can see how this benefits them. But the good salesperson asks questions to find out what the customer wants to use the barrow for. Then each customer is presented with a different benefit. For example, the good salesperson would target different customers in the following ways:

- Older person: 'Twin wheels mean the barrow is easier to control.'
- Farmer: 'The galvanised body means it won't rust, even when used for manure.'
- Builder: 'You won't get punctures from any nails lying around your site.'

Can you see how the same barrow appeals for different reasons to each person?

top tip

The price someone will pay for a product will largely depend on how it's going to be used. Packaged and presented differently, one product can be quite legitimately sold for different prices for different applications.

Which means…

The easiest way to get into the habit of presenting benefits and not just features is to say 'which means…'. This forces you to translate a feature into a benefit. If you can't find a suitable benefit, then the feature is of no value in this situation. For example:

- 'Our detergent is highly concentrated *which means* a litre will last a long time.'
- 'Our vegetable seeds are pelleted *which means* more will germinate.'
- 'We fly overnight *which means* you can have a day in the office before departing.'

building the business getting sales: shortcuts to closing deals

How to structure your sales pitch

A sales pitch should really be no more than a focused conversation. Focused because you want to see if the person you're with is going to buy! The fastest way to achieve this is by directing the conversation along a logical track, which runs as follows: attention–interest–desire–closing the deal.

Attention

In a showroom or exhibition environment, grabbing attention is a vital part of the process. If someone shows interest, you need to engage them in conversation.

- Do ask – 'What interests you most about... ?'
- Don't say – 'Can I help you?'

Interest

Having got their attention you need to ask open questions to find out what they're interested in and why. Key things to discover include:

- why they are interested
- what they would do with the product or service
- how valuable this would be, ideally in quantifiable terms
- what else they might be considering.

Desire

This is where you introduce some features and benefits to the conversation. Having identified the areas of greatest interest you now have the opportunity to introduce the benefits you can offer in terms that mean something to your prospective customer.

If you don't know enough to work out the tangible benefits, ask your prospect to help you. You don't need to have all the answers yourself.

Closing the deal

As you work through the benefits, it makes sense to check to see if your prospect is ready to buy. There's no rule that says you have to plough through every possible benefit. The right time to close the deal is when your prospect is ready.

To close the deal, you simply ask for the order. Or you can be more subtle and use phrases such as:

- 'So you think this will do the job then?'
- 'Would you prefer it in white or red?'
- 'Are you confident now that this is the right choice for you?'

A sales interview should not be a verbal combat. Subtlety sells, as does showing concern that the customer is sure they're doing the right thing. Subtlety gets results quicker.

Overcome objections

If people are not convinced, they will say no when you try to close the deal. However, no does not always mean no. It frequently means 'I'm not sure yet'.

When someone says no, ask them why. Or to be more specific, ask them:

- 'What concerns do you still have about this?'
- 'What makes you feel this is not right for you at the moment?'
- 'What would convince you to say yes?'

Questions like these prompt your prospect to tell you why they're not ready to buy yet. You can then deal with each issue in turn and ask for the order again.

Confirming what is agreed

Once you've got the order, you need to confirm the details of what's been agreed. This can save a lot of heartache later, as often people hear what they want to hear and not what you said. Some people use order forms and ask for a signature. What's vital is that you and your customer both have a record of what's been agreed.

building the business
getting sales: shortcuts to closing deals

Sales shortcuts

- ▨ Check that you're selling to someone with the authority to buy.

- ▨ Watch body language. When someone decides to say yes, they physically relax.

- ▨ If you're not sure what to say next, ask a question.

How to overcome objections

You have to help people over their normal instinct to delay saying yes. That's not to say you push; pushing smacks of insincerity, or worse, desperation. Instead give people every encouragement to say yes.

The way to ensure you identify objections is to try closing. You should always be closing (this is often described as the ABC of sales). To do this, you need to remain in control of the conversation. You have to direct it in the way you want it to go. You do this by using open and closed questions.

Open questions:

- ▨ usually start with what, why, how, where, when, etc.

- ▨ encourage your prospect to 'open up' and share information.

Closed questions:

- ▨ usually require a yes or no answer, or offer the choice between two options

- ▨ encourage your prospect to agree, disagree or make a choice.

So, in your conversation you use open questions to identify issues, attitudes and gather information. You then use closed questions to check that you've understood correctly or gain commitment. Here's how a conversation could sound:

> **Prospect:** *We have used the same fuel supplier for many years, but of late they have become a little unreliable.*

> **Salesperson:** *So perhaps they've become complacent. Tell me, what problems does that unreliability create?*

Prospect: *Well, we like to keep our fleet with their tanks topped up, but last week a delivery was late and so to avoid running out, we started fuelling each morning as the trucks went out.*

Salesperson: *And what problems does that create?*

Prospect: *Well, drivers forget and then have to stop at a filling station.*

Now if in this example you were selling fuel cards that enabled the prospect's drivers to fill up almost anywhere, at the same price as he was buying fuel from his unreliable supplier, and he didn't have to carry stock, you'd have a sale. Note the way the salesperson repeats key words from what the prospect says in the question that solicits more detail. This is called directive questioning. You can ask both directive open and closed questions.

By following this track, you can quickly get to the nub of the prospect's issues and identify the objections. If you don't retain control of the conversation, you'll struggle to identify objections. There are two kinds of objections.

Sincere objections are genuine barriers (in the prospect's mind) to a decision to buy. For example:

- 'I have no budget left for this year.'
- 'I really can't see myself wearing one of those.'
- 'I've never fancied driving a black car.'

Insincere objections are usually excuses or attempts to stall your attempt to get a sale. For example:

- 'It's too expensive.'
- 'I don't like it.'
- 'I'm busy and I need to get on now.'

You can usually tell what kind of objection you're hearing because:

- sincere objections tend to be specific and logical
- insincere objections tend to be unspecific and emotional.

building the business getting sales: shortcuts to closing deals

6

Successful salespeople recognise the difference between the two. They:

- ◪ stop the meeting and seek to remake the appointment if the objection is insincere – they know they won't get a sale today

- ◪ deal with each objection as it arises, gain agreement that it's been resolved and move closer to winning a sale.

golden rule

You need to become so proficient at directing conversation that you can lead your prospect through the sales process by instinct. People enjoy talking with good salespeople as it doesn't feel like they're being sold to.

How to create urgency

to ensure that people buy you need to create urgency

To ensure that people buy when you want them to buy you need to create urgency. Sometimes urgency is there anyway and just needs emphasising. At others you need to create it. Here are some examples.

Natural urgency

This exists when circumstances are changing and therefore immediate purchase makes sense. The most powerful examples of natural urgency are those created by nature itself. For example:

- ◪ you need to buy heating oil as the weather gets colder

- ◪ children need school uniforms when they reach school age

- ◪ farmers need fertiliser in spring when crops start growing.

Time urgency

This kind of urgency can be genuine or contrived. You use time urgency to get commitment to buy, as the customer appreciates that it will not be possible to come back and buy the same thing another time. For example:

- you can't buy a ticket for a train that's just left

- announcing a price rise next month makes buying this month more attractive

- you have a cancelled order to replace and can offer a discount for an immediate decision.

Creating scarcity

There are many reasons why scarcity occurs. Some are inevitable and some are contrived to maintain market price (for example oil supply). By suggesting that supplies are limited or even running out you create scarcity. For example:

- car makers discount stocks of an old model when a new one is launched

- a flight only has so many seats so if you book too late you can't travel

- commodities are often limited in supply so people are encouraged to buy options to secure their supply.

Don't be last to buy one!

A very strong emotional driver is the fear of being the last person in your community to adopt new technology or practice. History tells us that it's easy to be left behind, and nobody likes to be considered 'out of date'. Examples might include:

- your competitors staying in touch using Blackberries™ – are you missing out?

- kids always wanting to wear the latest fashions

- almost every house but yours having satellite TV.

building the business getting sales: shortcuts to closing deals

'Early adopters' and bargain hunters

Jamie is sales director of a copier company. He is the most effective salesman I know. He understands and remembers what drives each of his customers. Some like to keep up to date with the latest technology. Others are always receptive to a good deal. (I fall in the second group!)

When his early adopter customers buy the latest machine, he takes their used copier in part-exchange. He then sells those machines on to people like me who remain content with their current copier until Jamie calls. Jamie describes how the machine he's just taken in will make life better and provide new features. He always has other people he says are interested so it becomes a 'now or never' decision. Jamie's company is very successful.

top tip

You can sometimes make more profit from selling trade-ins than you do from selling a new machine. Always look at the margins you make along the length of the chain, not just at one deal in isolation.

Why you must confirm the deal

A sale is not a sale until the money's in the bank. Ask any long-term entrepreneur about the things that can go wrong with an order and they'll give you a long list. Customers go bust, die, change their minds or simply play difficult and complain about everything to reduce the price.

Savvy entrepreneurs protect themselves by confirming in writing exactly what's been agreed. In many situations, especially when selling to consumers, it's good to use an order form and have the customer sign to show their agreement.

You can confirm a sale by:

- writing a friendly letter to confirm what's been agreed
- sending an order form for the customer to sign and return
- asking for a purchase order (as large firms often won't pay unless the order number is quoted on your invoice).

Getting paid

Confirming the details of a sales order presents a golden opportunity to ask for payment. Do not assume that you have to wait for your money until after you've delivered the product or service.

Here are some top tips for getting paid:

1 Ask for payment in advance if it's a new customer – this is common practice.

2 Take a deposit with the order – many manufacturers do this.

3 Accepting credit cards enables your customers to pay you immediately.

4 Factor your debts – this means you effectively borrow against the invoice when it is issued, with the lender collecting the debt. You usually get around 80 per cent straight away and the balance, less their fee and interest, when the customer pays.

top tip

Consider paying someone, your bookkeeper for example, to chase payments for you. It saves you the trouble of doing it yourself and also means you can concentrate on selling.

Seeking feedback

As well as confirming your order, it is good practice to seek feedback when the deal has been completed, payment received and the product or service used.

You can do this by:

- phoning to ask how things were
- sending out a questionnaire
- inviting your customer to complete an online survey
- visiting them.

building the business
getting sales: shortcuts to closing deals

Gathering feedback is important because it:

- allows you to check customer satisfaction
- lets you find out about quibbles and problems you can solve
- gives you tips for product/service improvement
- provides a great opportunity to ask for the next order!

and finally...

Now think about:

- What are the benefits your customers value most?
- How can you use questioning to get to the sale quicker?
- When was the last time you asked a happy customer to introduce you to someone new?

getting online
bypass the hype and profit from the internet

- ◢ The reality of online marketing
- ◢ Managing your website's content
- ◢ Making money from online sales

An unattractive business proposition remains unattractive however many people have the chance to see it. Equally, a brilliant product or service can be bought by more people more readily via an online shop.

Don't make the mistake of thinking that a lacklustre business offer will look brighter on the internet – it won't.

Online marketing – the myth shattered

The internet can provide your business with many very effective shop windows. It's a great way to capture customers. You have to remember, though, that your business exists to do more than capture customers. You also have to be able to interact with them and make it easy for them to buy from you.

your business exists to do more than capture customers

You have to work harder at targeting your prospective customers online than you do via other mediums. With press advertising, direct mail and cold calling, you identify your prospect and make your approach, even if collectively. Online, you have to set out your virtual stall and wait for your customers to find you.

The myth that needs shattering is this: sales success is not directly proportional to audience size. Online marketing is not a numbers game at all.

Website principles

1 Your website can promote your business, or you, but not both. It's good to separate self-promotion from product/service promotion. Even if you're a sole trader customers will be more interested in what you do than who you are.

2 Almost everything you publish on the internet can be read by your customers, suppliers, staff and even your mum if she goes online. It's possible to spend large sums on web marketing and see that investment severely handicapped by inappropriate blogs elsewhere.

3 The internet is a 24/7 environment. People expect instant confirmation of any purchase and answers to questions in hours, not days.

the internet can magnify your opportunities and broadcast your threats

In other words, the internet can magnify your opportunities and broadcast your threats. It is, however, a place you have to be seen from the very beginning of your business.

Being found online

Search engines are constantly developing. Yesterday's brilliant wheeze for appearing higher up the search rankings might still be OK today. Tomorrow, it probably won't work at all. As fast as people find ways to trick search engines, so the search engines find ways to see through the bluff.

Things the experts tell me that have a lasting impact on the ease with which your website is found include the following.

- Being very focused about what you are promoting. Use a few things to capture interest, rather than trying to promote everything you do equally.

- Embedding within your website the phrases people might use to search for what you do. These can be incorporated within the page code or added as metatags. (It can be wise to pay someone to handle this for you. It's called 'search engine optimisation'.)

- The more links there are to your site from other, genuine sites and the more frequently you add new content, the easier the search engines find you.

top tip

Spend a few hours searching for your business online. Imagine you are a customer unaware of your business. Use the search phrases they might use. See what you can learn from the websites that this search identifies. Pay most attention to those that appear before your own.

Don't get hung up on domain names

It's the words on a website, the frequency with which it is updated and the links to it that generate traffic, not the domain name. The value of a domain name is in how it is remembered by people. In other words, the role of a domain name is to help people who know about you to look up your website. That's why most businesses choose website names that:

- are essentially their business name – in my case
  robertashton.co.uk

- describe their business activity in a generic way – for example, the B&Q website address is diy.com.

getting online: bypass the hype and profit from the internet

building the business

7

Domain name dos and don'ts

By accepting that your domain name is actually not crucial to your online success, the experienced entrepreneur will do the following.

- Buy a number of relevant domain names and have them 'pointed' to his or her website. This is low cost and makes good sense.

- Not be persuaded to buy lots of domains simply because they are there and unassigned. Few competitors will buy them if you don't so why bother?

- Consider buying a generic domain name if it is relevant and likely to generate positive publicity offline, for example, on press advertisements, product packaging and vehicle liveries.

- Stick to one website rather than several.

top tip

It's easy to get drawn into buying new web domains when they become available; for example your existing domain with a recently created suffix. The main beneficiaries of this exercise are the vendors.

Domain name checklist

When you buy a domain name bear in mind the following points:

1 Is it short, memorable and obviously linked to who you are or what you do?

2 Is it easy to remember? Avoid hyphens, underscores and potentially confusing letter/number combinations.

3 Does it mean the same as you intend in all languages/markets in which you sell?

4 Does it inadvertently infringe anyone's trademarks, etc.?

5 Does it contain words that might mean your emails get caught in spam filters?

6 Do you really, really need to buy it at all?

Ample Bosom

Sally Robinson is a Yorkshire farmer's wife. She created an online business retailing underwear for the larger lady. The idea came about because being a large lady herself, she found it hard to buy comfortable bras in her rural part of the country. Her business model was simple. She wanted to make it easier for larger ladies to buy underwear online. She stocks 200 sizes!

She chose a name for her business that was memorable, highly descriptive and in many ways very appropriate. To many people farmers' wives are large, buxom and motherly. Ample Bosom supports that vision on all fronts.

Because Sally has successfully gained lots of publicity for her business over the years, it has grown in both sales and value. Should she want to sell her business, she now has a very strong brand that could fit within a number of online retailers. Her domain name, which was probably cheap to buy, is now a key element in the value of her business: www.amplebosom.com.

Fast ways to manage website content and cost

It's easy to get confused when faced with so much choice. Your website can do so much, yet to be effective it needs to be focused and gradually evolve, with new content added regularly.

Content is king

The paradox of websites is that content is more important than appearance. It's what your site says that is important, not clever graphics. People are looking for content, not entertainment, when they visit a business website.

The content you add to your website need not be your own. The stuff you have discovered that is of interest to your audience can also be included. Be sure to credit the source and gain any permissions first though.

content is more important than appearance

building the business
getting online: bypass the hype and profit from the internet

Good content can build your reputation, build your network of contacts and win you business. For example, good content can:

- demonstrate that you know what you are talking about
- keep people informed about what you think and do
- promote your products/services
- recruit subscribers to your e-newsletters
- offer free guidance to people
- take and process orders
- form part of your back-office function
- be posted by visitors to your site in a user forum.

Managing content

Perhaps the most common mistake people make is to overlook the need to be able to update their website themselves. If you have to pay your web developer every time you want to change anything it will quickly drive you mad. For one thing they may not view updating your website as a priority task. For another they'll charge you to do it!

There are many very good content management systems around. Some of these are developed for specific markets. SubHub (www. subhub.com), for example, provides easy to self-manage websites for people who want to build audiences of paying subscribers. Others will focus on e-commerce and there are some 'open source' solutions you can use that will cost you nothing.

Adding content

Content management of websites can bring out the geek in all of us. It's easy to become fascinated by your website and spend lots of time working on it. If you're going to avoid being distracted, you need to be sure that the time you spend on your website could not be more usefully spent elsewhere.

Only add content that:

- ☑ you agree with
- ☑ has some value to your audience
- ☑ is not copyright.

Good content to add is:

- ☑ customer testimonial
- ☑ case studies
- ☑ pictures that illustrate the above.

top tip

If you're already busy, find someone with the time and skills to maintain your website for you. Agree with them a monthly activity schedule and encourage them to nag you to provide the content they need.

Managing cost

Your business's website is your shop window. It is also your shop and maybe even your cash register too! Having a good content management system means that your website costs are fixed.

A good website can save you money in the following ways:

- ☑ promotional brochures can be added as downloads
- ☑ you need less promotional print and save on postage
- ☑ customers can find information without having to ring you.

top tip

Set an annual budget for your web marketing and make sure you spend it all. Investment online is inevitably cheaper and can be more effective than other forms of promotion.

building the business
getting online: bypass the hype and profit from the internet

Easy ways to take money online

Taking money online is very satisfying. Imagine going to work on a Monday morning and finding that lots of people have placed orders, and paid for them, online over the weekend. Not every business can sell online, but most can.

taking money online is very satisfying

What to sell online

Some businesses appear more suited to online trading than others. Books and CDs are two of the most common consumer online purchases. Software, that you buy and then download, is a simple business purchase where you don't have to do anything – apart that is from write the software!

The hard-nosed entrepreneur will recognise that much of what is currently being given away for free can be sold. For example:

- solicitors can sell downloadable document templates
- machine makers can sell tools, filters and other consumables
- training companies can sell self-learning materials.

top tip

Packaging and presenting your knowledge in a simple format and selling it online enables you to sell to people who would not normally become your customers.

Take a look around the internet to see what others are selling that you currently give away. Then start selling too.

How to sell online

The only way to sell online is to accept payment by credit or debit card. You do see some websites that invite you to print out your order and post it with a cheque. Most people avoid these and find someone easier to buy from.

Accepting card payments is easy and does not cost as much as some people may lead you to believe. There are low cost options, such as Paypal™ and Worldpay™, but these specify 'small business' and may put some people off.

The confident entrepreneur invests a little more in a professional system that looks good, looks very secure and encourages people to buy. Few will volunteer their credit card details to a site that looks amateurish.

Here's how to do it. First, set up a merchant account with a bank. It doesn't have to be your usual business bank but ask them first. A merchant account puts in place the process to accept credit card payments. There are different types of account and fees apply to each. You need one that accepts online payments.

Second, set up an account with a payment gateway provider, such as www.protx.com. These provide the interface between your website and your bank account when your customer gets to the pay part of their purchase. The best ones offer a range of packages that enable you to upgrade as your business grows.

Next, create an online shop on your website. Some content management website providers build this into their package. Others use off-the-shelf packages such as Actinic™ software.

Once set up, it should cost you no more than £600 per year in fees until your online business becomes serious.

top online tips

- ◢ Simple is good. People buy what's going to help them. Things need not be complicated.

- ◢ Be free too. Offer people lots of free stuff. It shows them the quality of what you're selling.

- ◢ Save downloads in pdf or some other read-only format.

- ◢ Work on getting the search engines to find you easily.

- ◢ Make buying from you online easy to do.

building the business
getting online: bypass the hype and profit from the internet

and finally...

Now think about:

- What do you want your website to do – recruit enquiries or sell?
- Are you investing online or trying to do it on the cheap?
- What could you sell online?

get networking
shortcuts to spending more time with the right people

- ☑ How to network
- ☑ Where to network
- ☑ Manage your network

Why you need to network

Success is as much a result of who you know as what you can do. Most of us, when looking for a supplier of any kind, ask around for recommendations. It's a natural thing to do. You want to be a business that is recommended quite often so you need to be well known.

> you want to be a business that is recommended quite often

Successful entrepreneurs build and maintain extensive networks of contacts. It enables them to get things done fast. It also enables them to broker deals.

How to choose the right networks

Business networking is just like social networking only with different people. It's not complicated and the same rules apply. Think of it as a relationship spectrum, ranging from the intimacy of close family at one end to the colder, one-off business transaction at the other. Your networking relationships will be in the middle part of that spectrum. The skill is to make the relationships as broad as possible.

Good networkers:

- take a genuine interest in the people they meet
- offer people help unconditionally
- keep in touch
- introduce people within their network to each other
- follow up when opportunities come their way.

top tip

Think of your network as a bank account. You have to invest before you can hope to get any return.

Choosing networks to join

There are literally thousands of business networks. Most are keen to welcome new members. For the lone worker in a small business they provide valuable social contact as well as opportunities to gain business referrals.

business networks provide valuable social contact

The first decision you have to make is what you want from a business network. If it's social contact, comradeship and a regular get together to chat about common challenges and opportunities, then join a network that delivers that. However, you're unlikely to meet highly successful, seasoned entrepreneurs at a weekly breakfast networking meeting.

The best networks to join are those that:

- enable you to mix with people further along the business journey than you
- your potential customers attend
- will stretch your thinking and territory.

Before looking for networks to join, work out exactly what you want to achieve. Be honest with yourself. Consider in what proportions you want to:

- make new friends
- learn new things
- find new customers/suppliers.

Networks to consider

It's easy to assume that to do business networking you need to join a business network. This is not necessarily the case. Some of the most successful people never attend business networks; they network elsewhere.

Examples

An accountant becomes a charity treasurer to meet other charity Trustees (who tend to be people that use accountants!).

A business angel volunteers to judge a business awards programme to meet firms that might represent investment opportunities.

An animal feed maker joins a livestock club and becomes a show cattle judge.

Note that in each of the three examples, the individual is giving their time and expertise and doing something that raises their profile within the network.

Successful entrepreneurs know that the networks to join and become involved with are those populated with the right people. They know that traditional business networks are full of people wanting to sell, rather than people wanting to buy. In fact an early sign of success is when you find it impossible to sell at a networking event because everyone's trying to sell to you!

Consider joining networks such as:

- social clubs attended by your target customer groups
- trade associations that represent your customers

- debating societies that are attended by interesting people who will themselves know lots of people

- voluntary organisations that attract volunteers you'd like to meet.

golden rule

Networking is not about selling to the people you meet. It's about the people you meet being motivated to introduce you to people they know that might buy from you.

How online networking can save you money

There are literally thousands of online networks you can join. Many seek a modest monthly subscription and offer greater functionality in return. This can enable you to:

- post a profile of your business for others to see

- receive email alerts when someone checks out your profile

- use detailed search criteria to search the membership

- access forums where you can discuss topics with like-minded entrepreneurs

- access useful information posted by other members.

A good example is www.ecademy.com where, for a very modest monthly fee, you have access to thousands of people around the world. You can even click a button to find 'people like me', which presents you with a list of people who used the same key words as you in building their profile.

These online communities can be a huge distraction if you get drawn into contributing to the general chat that typifies them. If you are selective though, they can help you find people you would never otherwise meet. That can be incredibly useful.

Pinpoint recruitment through online networking

Steven's company manufactures equipment used in animal feed mills. He wanted to find someone to carry out a telephone survey of feed mill managers in Poland. Their attitudes to quality assurance would shape his strategy as he sought to increase his sales in Eastern Europe.

Using Ecademy he found three Polish-speaking market researchers. Each was invited to pitch for the work and one got the job. A bonus was that the successful bidder was actually based in Poland so was able to add much more to the project than if it had simply been one of a number of countries they covered. Both Steven and the researcher benefited. They would not have met had it not been for Ecademy.

Specific examples of how online networks save you money include the following:

- you can find new people fast – it's far easier to search a database than a room full of people!

- your choice is wider – virtual rooms hold more people than meeting rooms

- there's no travel and you can network online when it's most convenient for you

- it's fast – you don't have to waste time on small talk; you just go straight for the business opportunity.

But you have to know what you're looking for and be disciplined about it. There's always the danger of being distracted by the interesting detours and never reaching what you set out to discover.

Your online network profile

The better your online profile, the more likely you are to attract the interest of those you want to meet. As with any other form of marketing, you have to be focused. Although your profile will inevitably be as much about you as your business, everything it contains must emphasise the strengths of your enterprise.

It is vital that your online profile is:

- **explicit** – saying exactly what you do in language anyone can understand
- **honest** – depicting your business as it is now, not as you dream it will be in the future
- **human** – people deal with people and you need to appear approachable
- **illustrated** – in an online network, a good picture is vital – without it you're far less likely to be approached
- **current** – that what you're offering or seeking is clearly recently posted and up to date.

top tip

If you belong to an online network be sure to visit and check your profile at least weekly. Many show visitors to your profile when you were last logged on. If it was ages ago, they'll be less likely to think you're serious.

Why good networkers get remembered

Online or face to face, the best networkers are those who get remembered. You can be remembered for more than just your good points, so it's important to make it as easy as possible for people to remember you for the right reasons.

How you look

Most business networking events are packed with people wearing grey suits. Women as well as men seem to feel the need to 'look the part'. While you need to feel comfortable and not too outlandish, it is good to stand out from the crowd. At a networking event you want to be seen.

the best networkers are those who get remembered

Why you're there

If you go to a networking event 'to meet people and see who's there', you will not necessarily meet the right people. You need to be clear about what your business objectives are and what you hope to achieve from the time and perhaps money invested in the event.

top tip

If you can find out who else is attending before the event, reckon to spend as much time researching who you want to talk to as you will at the event itself. That way you arrive with a 'hit list'.

What you're after

If you go to a networking event and walk out with business in the bag, it means you're either very lucky or not ambitious enough. Remember that you're there to get referred, not to sell to everyone you meet.

It's also important to recognise the difference between a lead and a referral.

- A **lead** is a suggestion or a tip: 'John Smith might be interested in one of those, why don't you call him?'

- A **referral** is a solid introduction: 'Jane Jones might like one of those; give me your card and I'll mention it when I see her tomorrow.'

You can easily see which is the most powerful. But do be realistic!

A good first impression

When you meet someone for the first time, you need to make a good first impression. You do this by:

- smiling at them when you introduce yourself

- asking open questions and listening to what they say

- encouraging them to talk about themselves, not you

- not looking over their shoulder to see who you're missing.

Getting results

New networkers often go to an event, feel they've achieved little and give up. Those in the know realise that networking is a long-term project. You need to:

- build relationships with people
- build their confidence in your ability
- equip them to introduce you (always give new contacts a card)
- make introductions for them so they feel good about you.

Your elevator pitch

When you meet someone new you've got less than a minute to grab their attention. You do this by developing your 'elevator pitch'. It's what you'd say to someone if you literally were with them in a lift and only had a minute to persuade them to continue the conversation after they step out at the third floor.

A good elevator pitch follows this track:

1 Who you are – you start with your name.

2 What you do – describe in a few words the benefits your business activity delivers. For example, don't say, 'I run a garage.' Instead say, 'I look after people's cars so they don't break down.'

3 How you're different – you won't be the only person they've met in your line of business. Explain why you're different. For example, 'We have a monthly payment plan so our customers can spread the cost of car maintenance and avoid big bills.'

4 What you're looking for – if you don't say what you're hoping to find, the person you're speaking to won't know. So to continue using the example, 'We've just expanded and can accommodate more customers.'

If you have a good elevator pitch, people will remember you for it.

Why keep in touch?

Building business relationships is like building a wall. Once you've laid a firm foundation, you can keep adding new bricks without loosening the old ones. Over time, successful people build up their network of contacts and keep in touch with them all. Knowing lots of people is the quickest way to get things done. You always 'know someone who can'.

How to keep in touch

How often you are in touch with someone will to an extent depend on both them and you. Busy people (the best ones to know) will rapidly tire of frequent, seemingly needless communication. So it's most important that when you contact someone there's a reason. What's more, that reason has to benefit them as well as you.

When you have a small circle of people you want to keep warm in your network, it's quite easy to remember to keep in touch. Here are some examples of tried and tested techniques you might try.

Examples

- *Ring them up – email is convenient, but the telephone is more personal. Your voice will always be more appealing than your words alone. Phone people to ask how they are handling some current issue that might be bothering them. They'll almost certainly ask you how you're doing and that's your prompt to tell them!*

- *Post news cuttings – this works really well with professional services clients. You spot a press article that impacts on their sector, rip it out, add a handwritten note and post it to them. It flatters them that you're thinking of them. It also makes no demands, so is uncondi- tionally generous on your part. That matters too.*

- *Ask advice – you're planning something new. Perhaps you've drafted a leaflet or even produced some samples. Send them to people who may or may not be customers and ask for their feedback. The chances are that they'll both share their opinion and recommend some potential customers for what you're proposing.*

Some people are what is termed 'early adopters'. This means they like to be amongst the first to try anything new. Always identify the early adopters in your network and offer them opportunities to try new things.

Keeping in touch using technology

Once your network grows beyond the point where you can remember everyone easily, you need to invest in a database. There are a number of databases you can buy and use. They are called 'customer relationship management' (CRM) systems. Despite the name, these packages are for keeping in touch with all of your contacts, not just your customers.

With software to help you, it's easy to stay in touch. Good CRM software will:

- keep your contact details neatly in one place
- allow you to add notes from meetings/conversations
- prompt you when you've agreed to next make contact
- make it easy to mail-merge an email document
- integrate with your accounting software if/when they become customers.

The value of remaking contact

Lewis is a very successful investment adviser. He has an extensive network of contacts and keeps them all abreast of what's new in terms of opportunities.

One evening, as he called into a restaurant to book a table for later that evening, he spotted a former colleague across the room. He'd not spoken to the man for almost 15 years, yet remembered his name, walked across, introduced himself and left his card.

The next morning his former colleague received an email from Lewis and is now firmly on Lewis's radar as far as a sale is concerned. Successful people, especially those in a sales rich business like financial services, never hold back from making or remaking a new contact.

and finally...

Now think about:

◢ Who do you know that might be able to introduce you to new customers?

◢ How are you going to be more selective in where you network?

◢ How might you use software to make it easier to keep in touch with people who might matter one day?

get profitable
shortcuts to making more from each sale

- ☑ How to charge more
- ☑ How to sell more
- ☑ How to reduce your costs

Premium brands make more

It's easy to be cheap, but the most respected brands are the expensive ones. We make jokes about Skoda (or certainly used to) and aspire to driving a BMW or Mercedes. We pay a premium to eat in a classy restaurant and talk endlessly about the experience. We visit fast food outlets and once our hunger is sated, promptly forget them.

the most respected brands are the expensive ones

Successful entrepreneurs know how to create environments within which we happily pay more for their products and services. They focus as much on the intangible as the tangible. One thing they also have that the newcomer may lack is confidence. Confident people can always get away with charging more.

How to charge higher prices

Customers worry more about prices that look too low than they do about prices that look too high. In most people's minds, there's a price range for anything. If you're too cheap they'll question quality. Too expensive and they'll question value.

in most people's minds, there's a price range for anything

In general, the more someone wants what you have, the more they'll pay to get it. For example, ice creams always cost more on the beach than in the supermarket.

Price should always be related to the value added rather than cost of production.

Buying motives

A useful way of understanding how your customer sees value is to think in terms of 'buying motives'. A buying motive is a reason for buying. I buy a sandwich because I am hungry, a train ticket because I want to travel and a hotel room because I want to sleep; the more complex the purchase, the more complex the buying motive.

In general, people buy for both emotional and logical reasons; for example:

- emotional – 'I *want* one of those' – often experiences such as going to the cinema

- logical – 'I *need* one of those' – often physical such as groceries.

So to command a higher market price, you need to satisfy both emotional and logical desires. It's often said that the decision to buy is emotional, with logic used to justify the decision to yourself and others. For example:

- you need a car to get to work every day

- you want a car to enhance your image and reputation

- you need a car that is economical and retains its value

- you want a car that goes fast and makes you feel good.

There's a really useful mnemonic that people use to align their marketing message with their customers' likely buying motives. It's SPACED:

- **Safety** – how safe will this product be or how will it enhance my own security?

- **Performance** – what does it do and how well does it do it?

- **Appearance** – do I like the look of it and will it enhance my image to own/wear/use it?

- **Convenience** – how easy is it to buy and use? Can I take it out of the box and switch it on from the start, or must I read an instruction book?

- **Economy** – will it go a long way? Will it be expensive to run? Can I afford it?

- **Durability** – how long will it last? Is the supplier going to be there in the future to provide support?

People who charge higher prices know that presenting their product or service in SPACED terms makes it easier for the customer to see the value.

Here are two examples:

Buying motive	Life coach	Lawn mower
Safety	Keeps you on track	Has a circuit breaker
Performance	Glowing testimonials from satisfied clients	12 inch cut and powerful motor
Appearance	It's cool to have a coach	It's chunky and green and looks smart
Convenience	The coach comes to you	It has a retractable power cable
Economy	Five sessions for the price of four	Costs pennies an hour to run
Durability	Has been trading for years so likely to stay	Guaranteed for two years

In general, the more of these buying motives you can satisfy, the more people will pay a premium for what you are selling.

top tip

Don't forget that all you have to do to charge more is put up your prices. Sometimes we fear doing this; try adding 5 per cent and see who notices!

The fast way to calculate selling price

When you put together a business plan, you carefully detail all of your costs. You also look at your capacity to produce or deliver and work out what your selling price needs to be to cover your costs and make a profit.

The sum is easy to do and we all do it. The calculation goes something like this:

Profit per item = selling price – costs (materials + labour) – overhead costs/sales volume

Be careful because there are lots of costs you can easily forget that can conspire to turn your anticipated profit into a loss. These include:

- replacement costs of equipment that should be in the overheads
- the cost of borrowing money/late payment of invoices
- your own time, which needs to be in the overheads at a sensible figure, even if you don't pay yourself anything
- repaying your start-up loan, even if you had the money already and didn't need to borrow it.

You can include all this, calculate a price that gives you a good return and overlook entirely the market price. In other words, your starting price has to be what people will pay, not what it costs you to deliver. The challenge is to work with what the market will bear.

Market pricing

Opportunist entrepreneurs see the chance to make money when the market price is high and they can source what's needed at a low cost. Remember that the customer is buying what your product or service does, not what it is. Here's an example.

the customer is buying what your product or service does, not what it is

Sodium hypochlorite is a chemical more commonly called bleach. You can buy bleach in a one litre bottle or a fifty litre drum. It's a commodity that every supermarket or janitorial trade outlet stocks. However, bleach is also good at cleaning blocked drains. It dissolves the fats that cause them.

I recently bought a rather macho looking bottle that promised its contents could blast their way through a blocked sink. A close look revealed that the main constituent was bleach. So I paid a hefty premium over the price of regular bleach for a few low cost additives and a label that promised the product could fix a problem.

top tip

Problems add value as they create urgency. In this case the product offered an alternative to dismantling the plumbing and cleaning it out by hand.

You can often re-package or re-present products and services in ways that focus on a problem and sell at a premium price. Other examples include:

- accountants who position themselves as 'turnaround specialists', able to rescue your business when it's heading down the tubes
- motor mechanics who operate 'emergency roadside repair' services
- fizzy drinks high in glucose that are positioned as 'sports drinks' and claim to keep you going when you're competing in a race.

Your selling price

Naturally you need to calculate your break-even price based on what your products or services cost to deliver. But that is not the

building the business
get profitable: shortcuts to making more from each sale

9

price you sell at. Your selling price can be calculated by asking yourself the following questions:

- What's the minimum I can sell for and still make a profit?
- What's the price range in my marketplace (cheapest to most expensive)?
- Where does what I do add the most value to the customer?
- How can I enhance what I do to appeal especially to people in that situation?

Then you sell at your highest price.

top tip

Adding in a higher level of service can add more value to a product than you gain from investing more in the product.

How to survive a downturn

Economies move in cycles. You cannot have good times without the occasional downturn. The most important thing to remember is to keep things in perspective. Most economists accept that a recession exists when you experience two successive three-monthly 'quarters' of negative economic growth (for a more detailed look at surviving a downturn, see Chapter 16).

> you cannot have good times without the occasional downturn

Even in a downturn, many businesses continue to grow. However, recessions are unforgiving times and while the strong survive, the weak may not. The experienced entrepreneur will:

- understand that good times will follow
- avoid taking undue risks
- become stricter about collecting money
- keep everyone in the organisation motivated and avoid 'talking things down'.

Managing costs in a downturn

A predicted downturn should give you the prompt you need to thoroughly review your costs. Do not go through the list and simply cut out things you feel you can do without, such as staff training. This can be a false economy. But do look at:

- suppliers – to make sure you're getting the best deal
- sundries – those things you buy without really thinking about it, like stationery, fuel and those lattes!
- sub-contractors – could you do it cheaper in-house?
- temporary staff – has hiring temps for some tasks become a habit you can actually manage without?

Falling sales

Downturns can often mean a decrease in your sales turnover. It can also put you under pressure to reduce your prices.

top tip

Remember that if your output slows, so can your costs. If you sell the same volume at a lower price, your costs remain unchanged but your profit disappears.

When sales fall:

- increase your efforts to recruit new customers
- if you need to reduce your staff numbers do it quickly, compassionately and follow the rules stringently
- offer suppliers the opportunity to reduce their prices so you can in turn reduce yours.

Getting paid

Running a business is like driving a car. Even the best drivers can have someone pull out in front of them and cause a crash. In a downturn you need to become really vigilant and look out for approaching danger. A lot of good businesses go bust in troubled times because of bad debt.

building the business
get profitable: shortcuts to making more from each sale

9

Experienced entrepreneurs will work hard to protect themselves from bad debt. They will:

- seek more deposits and stage payments
- watch unpaid invoices and act promptly to chase
- set credit limits to restrict their exposure to bad debt
- take credit references before allowing new customers credit.

top tip

A downturn can be a good time to buy a business if you have the confidence, financial strength and expertise to weather the storm.

Innovation

Everyone looks to cut back on their expenditure when times are tough. Those same people tend to be ramping up their own sales efforts, which might seem to you to be somewhat contradictory.

When budgets are tight, smart entrepreneurs strip cost out of at least some of their range of products and services. This means they can offer an economy version and keep customers with them. It's better than being dumped!

Examples

- *A training company can focus course curricula to cover key points in less time, thus reducing the price.*
- *A machine maker can simplify the design to take away seldom-used features and launch a 'budget range'.*

Survival strategy becomes success story

Gerald was a small business consultant. He had a number of clients he worked with regularly, plus many more who hired him for the odd day. In the last recession, Gerald negotiated a modest monthly retainer with five of the businesses he worked with most often.

He agreed to meet each client once a month and provide a basic level of service that meant he was able to keep them on track on a fixed fee basis. This enabled him to weather a difficult two years and the five clients prospered.

When business started to boom once more, he recruited more clients on a similar basis, with a range of fee rates for different levels of support. What started as a survival strategy became a positive point

The quickest way to make more from each sale

It's almost always more profitable to sell more to the customers you have already than to find new customers. It's quicker to introduce an extra product or service to someone who's already a customer.

It's also easy to throw in for free things people would pay for. These might include:

- immediate delivery rather than next week
- pink instead of blue (even if both colours cost you the same)
- helpline support.

Selling extras

It's also important to sell extras. These can be more profitable than the original sale. In some business sectors, this can be quite easy. For example:

- hairdressers sell hair care products to their client in the salon
- computer dealers sell maintenance contracts
- a restaurant encourages you to have side dishes, dessert and coffee
- coffee shops sell squirts of flavoured syrups.

In other sectors this might need more creativity. For example:

- accountants sell insurance that covers the cost of a tax inspection
- business-to-business magazines sell graphic design services to advertisers
- airlines sell hotel accommodation.

In each case, the additional products and services add profit to the supplier and value to the customer.

Why extras are so profitable

Once you've exhausted your own supply of 'add-on' sales – the things you can easily provide – it makes sense to look more widely. Let's explore the example above of the airline.

As soon as the customer books an airline ticket you know where they're going, for how long and when. The hotels, car hire firms, tourist attractions and shops do not have access to that information. To reach your customer without your help, they have to advertise widely. That's an expensive process that you can shortcut.

When the airline offers its customers car hire and hotel accommodation, it rightly earns a generous commission. It's cheaper for the hotel and car hire firm than advertising and they only pay out when they get a sale. What's more, the passengers probably need to find a hotel anyway. They see these extras as a useful and convenient service.

How to identify extras you could sell

We all rightly tend to concentrate on our own product or service. It's easy to lose sight of the context within which it is used. Yet for the customer, context is everything. Think about:

- what prompts the purchase of what you're selling
- what else might be happening at the same time.

This not only helps you to identify extras, it also gives you a better understanding of what motivates your customer. Both are helpful.

Then ask yourself:

- What else does the customer need?
- Can I supply it myself?
- Who can I introduce and make a margin?

The Limes guest house

Pete and Gwen run The Limes. It's a pleasant six roomed guest house in a rural market town. All rooms are en-suite and their clientele tend to be retired couples interested in the heritage of the area.

When visitors ring to book a room, Peter asks what has attracted them to the area. He then offers to tailor their break for them, including as much or as little as they want. Experience tells him that this is best done over a cup of tea when people arrive.

He offers to:

- *organise a taxi from the station when they arrive*
- *book restaurants and theatre tickets*
- *arrange visits to places you can't normally visit (private gardens, etc.)*
- *book 'walking tour' guides of the town.*

His guest house has become very popular. People know they'll have all the help they need to experience the very best the area can offer. Peter and Gwen make on average 20 per cent more than they would from simply providing B&B.

and finally...

Now think about:

- How can you move your business upmarket?
- Why do people buy from you? What are their motives?
- What else could you most easily sell to your existing customers?

building the business
get profitable: shortcuts to making more from each sale

being popular
shortcuts to social responsibility

- The payback from putting back
- How to do cost-effective social responsibility
- Profitable partnering with charities

Why it pays to put something back

Every business transaction has to benefit all parties. That way they will all want to do it again. Demonstrating social responsibility as an entrepreneur should be treated like any other business transaction; in other words, it should be of benefit to everyone involved.

This means that you don't exploit anyone however tempting it might be. Being socially responsible means that you:

- take a long-term view rather than simply trying to make a quick buck
- recognise and value your firm's relationship with its neighbours, the environment and wider community

⬛ appreciate that investing some of your profits in the community that helped you make those profits will make doing business with you more appealing.

Knitting aid

Mary runs a wool shop in a small Scottish town. As much a hobby as a business, her shop is popular with the many older ladies who enjoy nothing more than to meet up for a knit and natter.

Every autumn she visits the local primary school and teaches a group of youngsters how to knit. She gives them needles and wool to knit blanket squares. The finished blanket is then sent to an aid charity.

Every knitter in the town knows about this venture. Many are grandparents of the children Mary is teaching. They bring in their odds and ends of wool for the annual blanket knit. None would dream of buying their wool anywhere else.

Even the simplest things can make a huge difference. In Mary's case, she is giving some time and materials away. In return she has a brilliant reputation as well as encouraging a new generation of knitters. Advertising could never deliver her the same kind of return on investment.

Spotting the opportunity

The business objective is to raise your profile and help people see that profit is not your sole motive (even if it really is!). Big organisations have charity and social responsibility (CSR) policies, budgets and teams. They might even have their own charitable trust that makes grants from income derived from invested profits.

The smaller business has to do it differently. Here's how:

1 Understand who your customers are and what influences them.

   I make wall-mounted letter boxes that sell via DIY sheds.

2 Think about what you can do for them that costs little and achieves a lot.

I want to link my letterboxes with good practice so I will consider running a 'Postman of the Year' competition.

3 Work out the impact on the business now and in the future.

I have an in-house marketing and PR person who can link this with an existing distributor support programme. DIY sheds give out entry forms.

4 Estimate the likely return on that investment.

The publicity I attract within DIY stores means they'll carry more of my stock and more letterboxes will sell.

5 Do it.

The scheme is launched in regional and national media read by my target (customer) audience.

6 Measure it.

Measure the increase in sales against the cost of the campaign.

Why some firms buddy with a charity and what it gives them

Every enterprise receives countless requests for support from good causes. It's the first place a local fundraiser looks. Schools also always seem to be fundraising. Mary's wool shop gives an example of how you can deal with schools.

As with your suppliers or customers, it makes sense to have a long-term, mutually rewarding relationship with a charity. This means it becomes part of your business strategy. It also means you have a good reason for turning down the rest!

Will it work?

Although a charity will usually ask you for money the opportunities are far greater. You need to start by looking at the fit between your organisations. Ask yourself these questions:

- Does the cause interest me and do I think it's worthwhile? (Because, for it to work, you have to become passionate about the cause.)

- Am I doing it for the right reason? (Or are you being urged to support something close to an employee's heart but not yours?)

- Is the charity well run, sustainable and meeting a genuine need? (Charities like businesses can be well or badly managed.)

- Will it influence my business profile? (It should win you publicity, endear you to customers and build staff commitment.)

- Is it going to be manageable or distracting? (Your business has to gain, not suffer.)

top tip

Rather than wait to be approached make enquiries and find a charity partner yourself. If you make the approach you're better able to create the kind of partnership you need.

What's possible?

In short, almost anything is possible. You and the charity CEO need to agree some common objectives to aim for. These need to be as broad as possible. It is often useful to create a matrix of activity and opportunity. For example:

Charity needs	Business has	Business needs	Charity has
Money	Products/services	Added value	Added value
CEO mentoring	An entrepreneur, you!	Broader perspective	Different challenges
Money	Customers	Corporate event	Theme for event
Materials	Unwanted materials	Publicity	A story
Volunteers	A workforce	Motivated workforce	Teambuilding opportunities
Office space	Spare office	Publicity	A story

There is no limit to what you can do if you think beyond the obvious at the outset.

Examples

■ *A bottled water company donates a percentage of its sales income to a water aid project in Africa. The project is promoted in the company's advertising and on its labels. When a new well is sunk in Africa, there's usually some press coverage. Water is a hard-to-differentiate product. People buy this company's water because they know it helps others.*

■ *A business that provides bulk soil, sand and peat for golf course and other landscaping projects wanted to stage a corporate event. The business owner knew that people would be reluctant to come to his yard for a barbecue yet wanted them to see the size and scale of his business. He made the barbecue a fundraising event for his local hospice. His customers not only came along but they brought their friends too. They also paid for their tickets, covering the business's costs and raising a considerable sum for the hospice.*

■ *A restaurateur wanted to generate publicity for his business. He could not afford advertising and wanted to do something different. With a local school he developed both a 'food miles' campaign and a cookery competition for students. The associated publicity emphasised his commitment to using local produce. It also attracted new business to his restaurant.*

What fundraising does for staff morale in the best places to work

There are many differences between entrepreneurs and employees. One is their differing attitudes to the company's bottom line. The entrepreneur knows that a good proportion of this is for him or her to spend one day. The employee sees profit simply as something that underpins their job security.

fundraising is a good way to motivate people to do that bit more

Profit sharing schemes can make employees more interested but rarely to the extent the business owner might like. Once someone is comfortable with their pay more money is never as big a motivator to work harder as you would think. Fundraising is a good way to motivate people to do that bit more.

building the business
being popular: shortcuts to social responsibility

Adopting a charity

In previous pages we have seen how a business and a charity can form a mutually valuable partnership. However, sometimes all the entrepreneur wants to do is to motivate the team. This can be remarkably simple to organise. Here's how:

1 **Choose a cause** – ideally with some link to your business but more probably something your people choose themselves. Encourage them to set up a charity committee to discuss and agree on a cause to support.

2 **Limit the time** – because the decision will not have been unanimous and new opportunities are always emerging. Many entrepreneurs have a charity of the year.

3 **Invite the charity in** – to talk at a team meeting about the work they do and how the money raised will be used.

4 **Set a target** – encourage your team to set a target. Many entrepreneurs then agree to match what the team raises from company profits.

5 **Let them plan what they're going to do** – within reason, make company resources available to them.

6 **Support the campaign** – offer help and advice along the way. Don't take over, though, as this is one situation where you're not the boss.

7 **Celebrate success** – in a way they're not expecting. Make sure you also get press coverage.

Team building through charity work

Susan runs her own insurance brokerage and employs 10 people. They specialise in motor insurance for unusual vehicles and also for young drivers.

Every January her team chooses a charity of the year. A window display in their high street shop publicises the choice and there are collecting tins on each adviser's desk. The team organises a range of events throughout the year, including a quiz night and a sponsored walk. They usually raise about £5,000. The cheque presentation is usually featured in the local paper.

Since introducing a charity of the year Susan has found her team works together far better, with fewer arguments. Working together for a non-work cause seems to help no end.

top tip

Introduce a payroll giving scheme that allows your team to become regular donors. Remember that Gift Aid enables the tax on that income to be reclaimed to boost the amount raised.

A more ambitious approach

Larger firms often choose to set up a charitable fund and make a number of grants each year. This can be complicated to set up but does enable employees to:

- take ownership of fundraising for a variety of causes
- set up their own grants panel and attract applications
- visit charities they've supported to see the impact of their giving.

Creating a company charitable fund means that money raised in different ways, for example fundraising, company giving and product related campaigns, can be put in the same pot. This can become very tax efficient for the company and its employees.

A managed charitable fund

Christopher is senior partner in a large firm of accountants. Their branches all do their own thing in terms of fundraising and the firm matches what they raise up to an agreed limit.

Rather than create their own charitable fund, the money is invested for them by their local Community Foundation. For a modest fee of 10 per cent of the grant money given out, the Foundation invites applications and deals with the administration of their giving. The Foundation also advises the firm's grants panel so that they make informed grant making decisions.

building the business
being popular: shortcuts to social responsibility

How to say no without causing offence

In the first year or so of a new business many entrepreneurs find themselves handling larger amounts of money than they've ever handled before. In the euphoria of newfound success, saying yes to requests for support seems easy. Only when you add it all up do you realise quite how generous you've been and how little you have to show for your philanthropy.

the way to say no to the casual approach is to have a clear policy

That's why it's a good idea to have a plan and some structure to your charitable activity. In fact the way to say no to the casual approach is to have a clear policy. Publishing your giving strategy on your website, or having a standard 'sorry but no' letter, that points out why you're saying no, can save you a lot of hassle.

> **The paradox of giving**: *The more you give the more you will be asked to give. Fundraisers target generous people!*

Tricks of the trade

Fundraisers with you in their sights will work hard to hook you and reel you in. They'll flatter you endlessly in their quest for support. Here are a few of the tricks of the fundraiser's trade.

- Meet you via a friend: it's a well-known fact that new donors will say yes to a friend more readily than to a professional fundraiser. That's why fundraisers are eager networkers. They know that the best way to new donors is via the people whose support they've already recruited.

- Seeing is believing: this is the phrase used to describe the visits you might be invited to make to a worthy cause. Actually meeting a charity's beneficiaries really tugs at the heartstrings and brings the ask to life.

- Fundraising events: an invitation to buy tickets for a black tie charity ball might sound affordable. Remember that during the evening there may be raffles, collections or auctions to increase your contribution. Some charities organise very prestigious events with impressive guest lists and top flight entertainers. The wealthy entrepreneur can easily part with thousands of pounds at one of these events. Attend with your eyes open and a budget in mind.

Tricks to watch out for

You'll also encounter fundraising campaigns that are not quite as good for your organisation as you might first think. These often involve you being invited to sponsor or advertise in a diary, calendar or year planner. These are then printed and distributed to people the organiser will claim are your potential customers.

But beware – these schemes:

- do not always have the full support of the charity being supported
- rarely give you a good return as recipients of the diaries (or whatever) are often not quite your target market
- are often hugely lucrative for the company promoting them. In other words, it's a good business and less than you think of your donation might find its way to the charity you want to support.

top tip

Your own fundraising ideas will always be better for you than those that others put in front of you.

and finally...

Now think about:

- How can you raise your profile in your marketplace?
- What charities do you know that you could partner?
- When did you last agree to support a cause and wish that you hadn't?

managing
the business

managing money
shortcuts to a healthy cash flow

- ▨ What to watch and why
- ▨ Why cash flow is all about timing
- ▨ How to get paid faster

There are two main causes of business failure. One is poor management; the other is running out of money. Cash really is the lifeblood of any business. As a business grows it needs more cash to maintain itself. Grow too fast without sufficient cash and your enterprise will die.

The figures to watch and why

Bank managers have that canny knack of looking at a pile of management accounts, doing some quick sums and then making some very astute comments about your business's financial health. Once you know where to look, you too can keep your finger on your financial pulse without being an accounting expert. It's easy when you know how.

> cash really is the lifeblood of any business

Here's a simple example to make it all understandable.

The company

Our example company makes wooden rolling pins. These are turned on lathes from purchased timber and then sold to retailers to sell on. The products are sold in packs of 20 at a price of £30 per pack. Retailers then sell the rolling pins to customers at £3.00 each. The business has an annual turnover of £360,000.

Here are some monthly figures:

Sales	1,000 packs = £30,000
Timber purchase	£10,000
Labour cost	£10,000
Overhead costs	£5,000
Cash in the bank	£5,000
Timber stocks	£4,000
Customer invoices sent but not paid	£45,000
Supplier invoices received but not paid	£16,000

How secure are you?

A business needs to have enough money to meet its commitments in the short term. It also needs to be able to meet any long-term demands, but often has assets against which these can be offset. For example, a business mortgage is not a problem if the building is worth more than the outstanding debt.

Here are some ratios you can easily work out.

Current ratio

This is simply your current assets divided by current liabilities. So in our example it is:

$$\frac{\text{Outstanding invoices} + \text{stock} + \text{money in the bank}}{\text{Unpaid supplier invoices} + \text{the month's wage bill}}$$

or

$$\frac{45,000 + 4,000 + 5,000}{16,000 + 10,000}$$

$$= \frac{54{,}000}{26{,}000}$$

So the current ratio is 2.07. This is very healthy as clearly you can pay your bills.

Quick ratio

This is the current ratio but with stock taken out of the equation. It's a better guide as stock cannot always be turned readily into cash. If you use no other ratio in your enterprise, this is the one to remember:

$$\frac{\text{Outstanding invoices} + \text{money in the bank}}{\text{Unpaid supplier invoices} + \text{the month's wage bill}}$$

or

$$\frac{45{,}000 + 5{,}000}{16{,}000 + 10{,}000}$$

$$= \frac{50{,}000}{26{,}000}$$

So the quick ratio is 1.9.

As a rule of thumb, the quick ratio needs to be more than one. If it's less than one, even 0.9, then seek advice.

There's one other important ratio to understand.

Debtor days

This gives you a measure of how quickly your customers are paying you on average. Late payment can damage your cash flow because you can't spend what you've not yet collected from customers.

Debtor days is:

$$\frac{\text{Outstanding invoices}}{\text{Annual sales}} \times 365$$

managing the business
managing money: shortcuts to a healthy cash flow

128

So using our example again it is:

$$\frac{45,000}{360,000} \times 365 = 45 \text{ days}$$

In other words, customers are on average taking 45 days to settle their invoices. Bank managers use this ratio to check how good you are at collecting debts.

Getting paid on time

When you start your first business, you are painfully aware of your shortcomings. You know what you could do better and sometimes breathe a sigh of relief when the customer says yes. Sending an invoice is almost embarrassing and chasing the money a step too far.

Instead, you print out and post statements and reminders, perhaps putting stridently coloured 'overdue please pay' stickers on the reminder to hasten the process. To the seasoned buyer, all of these are symptoms of a lack of confidence. They then put your invoice to the bottom of the pile.

Myth: Asking for the money makes it harder to ask for more business.

asking for the money is the perfect time to ask for more business

The opposite is true. Asking for the money is the perfect time to ask for more business. It's an integral part of your management of the customer relationship. You appear more businesslike if you discuss payment.

How to get paid

The experienced entrepreneur knows that the best way to get paid is to ask. It really is that simple. Over time you learn that the more opportunities you create for people to pay, the more likely they are to oblige.

Here are some tips you can follow.

- Pre-payments can be encouraged by:
    - accepting credit/debit cards (vital if you trade online)

- making it clear that you expect part or full payment in advance.

■ Payment on delivery can be encouraged by:
  - encouraging your staff to ask for money
  - asking for payment when the job is finished and the customer's satisfaction has been checked – people are most excited about anything new when they first experience it.

■ Early payment can be encouraged by:
  - putting 7 or 14 day terms on the invoice, rather than the standard 30
  - offering an incentive to pay quickly, ideally by offering something other than a discount.

■ Prompt payment can be encouraged by:
  - phoning to make sure the customer is happy with what's been delivered
  - phoning the person who pays the bills to make sure your invoice is 'in the system', before the date it's due
  - quickly resolving any problems or complaints.

Challenging convention

Business convention suggests that you do the job, send an invoice, then wait a month for payment. But there are no rules that say this is how it always has to be. For example:

■ when you book a holiday you always pay before you travel

■ you always pay for your meal before leaving the restaurant

■ many mail order companies insist on 'cash with order' and tell you to allow 28 days for delivery

■ house builders usually take a hefty deposit to reserve a plot.

In each of these examples the customer is paying you before you have to pay your suppliers. It is what's called 'positive cash flow'; the money flows in before it needs to flow out.

Providing you make it easy for people to do and understand, there's no reason why you should not take money up front

managing the business
managing money: shortcuts to a healthy cash flow

11

yourself. All you have to do is make it clear, make it relevant and make it easy.

Positive cash flow becomes profitable

Stuart started a painting and decorating business. He worked on his own and, having worked out what materials he needed, asked the customer either to buy them or to pay him to buy them before he started the job. He could not afford the outlay and was happy simply to be paid for his time.

As his business grew, he started bulk-buying paint and brushes but still asked his customers to buy these in advance. He delivered them at the start of a job and left any residue with the customer for touching up.

What started as a necessity helped when the business grew and eventually gave him an additional source of profit.

Quick ways to deal with overdue invoices

There's no such thing as a good reason for delaying payment. The excuses you hear will range from the ridiculous ('I've lost the chequebook') to the lame ('We only pay once a month and it was yesterday').

there's no such thing as a good reason for delaying payment

One thing experience teaches you is that there is only one genuine excuse for not paying an invoice on time. That is the fact that there isn't enough in the bank to allow the cheque to clear. In fact when someone is honest enough to tell the truth and their plight is genuine, most creditors will help.

top tip

If you find you can't pay your bills, be honest and tell people. Keep them informed and pay instalments as and when you can.

Asking for money

If an invoice remains unpaid a week after the agreed payment date you are perfectly entitled to ask why.

Confident, experienced entrepreneurs ask for the money:

- politely – listening to what the customer has to say
- assertively – you can't agree all the time; you want the money
- constructively – seeking a solution, not confrontation.

Then make a note of what you've agreed and email to confirm it. For example, if you are told something like, 'It's been a tough month but I can give you half next week and the rest at the end of the month' confirm this in writing. Then, if payment is a day late, ring the customer to remind them of the commitment made – or perhaps resend the earlier email that confirms what you agreed. Be persistent and polite.

Sending statements

Some big organisations only pay invoices when they receive a statement summarising the month's transactions. Find out whether this is the case, and if statements are needed, send them.

Calling round for the money

If someone is habitually promising and not delivering, it sometimes helps to visit them. Be aware that people plagued by debt can become very devious. Do not get yourself into a situation that could be interpreted later as threatening. This is more an issue when you sell to householders than in a business-to-business context.

However, visiting someone who is proving difficult to get payment from can:

- prompt them into writing you a cheque
- allow you to see how busy they seem (if a business)
- allow you to see how prosperous they appear.

Taking legal action

Taking people to court to recover debts is painful, protracted and emotionally draining. The paperwork, particularly for small claims, is simple enough, but probably not the best use of your time. Using a solicitor can both show that you are serious and save you the trauma of dealing with it yourself. Successful entrepreneurs are usually too busy making money to delve into the detailed work needed to take someone to court.

top tip

Unpaid invoices are often the result of a dispute. It's often better to negotiate a reduced sum for immediate settlement than waste time battling it out. Do a deal and move on.

A slippery customer

Reg was a smooth operator. He drove nice cars, wore smart clothes and sold timeshare apartments in the sun. He ran events in hotels to promote his business and recruit customers. A marketing company was hired to produce glossy brochures and advertising.

The payments Reg made to the marketing company never quite tallied with the invoices. He might owe £5,375 and pay £4,000. This was confusing and rather annoying but it was tolerated as he was a big spender.

Then the gap grew to just over £10,000. The marketing company directors started to worry. They tried to be firm with Reg but he simply fobbed them off with excuses.

Then the phone rang. It was one of Reg's team. Reg had died unexpectedly of a heart attack the day before. Time revealed that any money he'd had was cleverly concealed offshore. The marketing company never got paid.

and finally...

Now think about:

- What steps can you take to get paid sooner?
- How do you currently deal with late payers?
- Who could you ask to help chase payments if you find it difficult?

get legal
protect yourself from risk

The golden rules of business

Rules are strange things. Some of us feel compelled to follow them and actively seek out preordained, approved ways to do things. Others blithely rush about oblivious to any rules and never seem to get caught out. The savvy entrepreneur steers a middle route between these two extremes.

In the final analysis though, there are just three rules you have to remember:

1 Don't break the law in any way as it can land you in deep trouble.

2 Don't exploit your customers.

3 Never take a risk that can wipe out your business.

We will look at each one in some detail as there are important principles that you need to fully understand. We'll also look at a fourth type of rule – self-imposed regulation.

Don't break the law

There are laws and laws. Think of running your business like you drive your car. Do you always stick rigidly to the speed limits? Do you never park on a double yellow line for five minutes as you post some letters or get cash from an ATM? Most drivers seem to think it's OK to go a little over the limit, but would never drink and drive. Be pragmatic as you interpret business laws and regulations. If in doubt, seek advice.

Don't exploit the customer

In extreme cases, customer exploitation *is* illegal. You can go to prison if you defraud your customer or knowingly sell them dangerous goods. However, more likely is that you get tempted to cut corners, overcharge, underdeliver or otherwise rip the customer off in some way. Like elephants, customers never forget. And unlike elephants, customers can talk!

Never take a risk that can wipe out your business

A common definition of an entrepreneur is that he or she is someone who 'takes a financial risk in the hope of financial gain'. All business is about risk. You buy stock, advertise

all business is about risk

and hope to sell your products, services, time and expertise at a margin. However, risk has to be manageable. You wouldn't last long in Las Vegas if you put all your chips on one square on the roulette table. You might win a fortune but you're more likely to lose your shirt.

Self-imposed regulation

Most of us are our own worst enemy when it comes to imposing rules. The self-help gurus talk about 'self-limiting beliefs', things we think we can't do but perhaps have never tried. Entrepreneurship is all about doing what you didn't know was possible!

In our minds, though, we do store away perceptions and memories that somehow turn into rules. It's comfortable to define boundaries and that's one reason we all do it, even unwittingly.

Examples

- *A shopkeeper finds that most shoplifting is done by schoolchildren so assumes that all children are shoplifters and bans them. Most are not: they are potential customers with pocket money to spend.*

- *A small business owner cold calling to find new customers gets sworn at by a solicitor's receptionist. Rattled and upset, the decision is taken never to approach a solicitor again.*

- *My father always said that Ford cars were poorly built and unreliable. However, it's more than 25 years since he died and actually, Ford cars are very good. Why then do I still tend to avoid Ford cars?*

top tip

Only follow the rules you know will matter to you and others. Check the others out before blindly following them.

Risks that face the entrepreneur

Running your own business exposes you to risks you've never encountered before. The potential pitfalls are countless. Here are some you might look at first.

Your personal income

Employees take their monthly salary cheque for granted. They enjoy considerable job security and the protection of employment law. Most feel that their income is secure and so live life to the full. As an entrepreneur, you don't have that safety net.

This is what you need:

- Emergency funds – it can take a couple of years to build income from a new business to the level where it pays you regular monthly amounts. Stash away at least three months' living expenses, ideally more. The last thing you want to worry about in a crisis is paying household bills.

managing the business
get legal: protect yourself from risk

- Life insurance – if an employee dies, their partner usually gets three times their salary (or similar) from the employer's insurer. If you have your own business, you might want more cover, not less. Arrange it!

- Permanent health insurance – in part replaces your income if you're long-term sick. This kind of insurance pays you an agreed basic monthly sum after one, three or six months of illness. It can give you tremendous peace of mind.

Employment law

There are no employment laws to protect the sole trader. Working on your own you both create and tolerate your own workplace. You cannot sue yourself for wrongful dismissal if your enterprise fails!

However, as soon as you start to employ people, you have to comply with employment legislation. But, again, you personally are clearly not protected in the way your staff are.

When your business becomes a company, with a board of directors as well as managers and workers, things change again.

you cannot sue yourself for wrongful dismissal if your enterprise fails

Shareholders can hire or fire directors and, if you've diluted your shareholding to bring in investors, you can be victim of a boardroom coup. At this point you are once more an employee.

Becoming self-employed, then, means you are no longer protected by employment law until you have created your own corporation.

Other personal risks

As well as losing the security of employment and the protection of employment legislation, there are other risks facing the entrepreneur. Again these are risks your former colleagues may never encounter and may seem daunting to you at first. These include:

- losing your savings – you are investing your own money in your business not someone else's

- bank guarantees – money you borrow is always secured against something, usually your home, which means the bank could sell your house in a worst case scenario

- litigation risk – if you or your business are found to be responsible for damage, personal injury or similar loss, you can be sued. It's why you need insurance (see next section).

The insurances you need most

Every business, however small, needs insurance. The extent to which you protect yourself against things going wrong largely depends on you. If you're someone who worries you will buy more cover than if you're a more laid-back person. Whatever your viewpoint, you want to get the best possible deal.

Here are some types of insurance most businesses buy and how the experienced make sure they're getting the best deal.

Life insurance

Look back at page 138 to see why this is important for you. It's also good to provide it for your staff. They are, after all, employees and expect this as a benefit. Here's where to look for cover:

- Your bank will try hard to sell you insurance. They often insist you take out life insurance to cover any loans. They also usually have insurance sales targets to reach. Buying insurance from your bank might be easy but it's not always the cheapest.

- An independent financial adviser (IFA) will be bound by industry regulations to make sure they only sell you what you need. They will look at the whole picture and propose something accordingly.

- You can also often buy life insurance online. This might be cheaper but you have to know what you want. There's no advice and no comeback if you get it wrong. Read the small print.

Business insurance

There are many specialist business insurance brokers you can talk to. Trade associations, business and professional networks often have special member deals. Recognise that different providers specialise in different areas. You need to consider the following points:

What it's called	What it does
Public liability	Protects you from potentially massive claims if you unwittingly cause a disaster
Employer liability	Covers your liability for your employees (permanent and temporary)
Motor insurance	This *must* specifically cover the use of your vehicle(s) for business purposes
Product liability	Pays out should your products be proved to have caused damage or injury
Buildings insurance	What it says! If you rent, your landlord will pay this but you need to check
Office/workshop contents	Like your home insurance only for work
Glass and signs insurance	Shop windows and signage are often excluded from business insurance – they may need extra cover
Engineering insurance	Pays out if breakdowns, power cuts, etc. stop you from working
Pollution risk insurance	Covers you against the consequences of accidental pollution, for example effluent leakage into rivers
Professional indemnity	Protects you should a client sue you for the consequences of bad advice

As you can see, you can insure almost any risk – at a price. The smart entrepreneur makes sure he or she:

- buys the insurances you have to have (public, personal liability and motor)
- buys the additional insurances important to the specific business
- keeps an open mind about other insurances which might be expensive and cover low risk issues.

Expect the unexpected

Cedric was an avid stamp collector. When offered early retirement, he opened a small shop supplying stamp collecting equipment and buying/selling collections. It didn't make much money, but he also had his pension so was happy enough.

Naturally cautious, Cedric made sure every aspect of his business was fully insured against every conceivable risk. This gave him huge peace of mind.

Then his wife was badly hurt in a car crash. The other driver was not insured and she was unable to claim compensation. Cedric had to close his shop to look after her.

The moral of this case study is simple; however much insurance you buy, the unexpected can always catch you out. Be realistic!

Why litigation rarely pays

Litigation is what happens when you have a dispute with someone and can't settle it out of court. Litigation relates to civil, rather than criminal, matters – or, in other words, anything the police aren't interested in prosecuting themselves.

the main beneficiaries of litigation are the legal firms that pursue it

As you might imagine the main beneficiaries of litigation are the legal firms that pursue it. The lawyers get paid whatever the consequence of the action. They are often the only real winners.

Why litigation happens

More often than not litigation happens because two people won't back down and seek an agreement. They become emotionally embroiled in their dispute and choose to use solicitors to fight a battle on their behalf.

The smart entrepreneur, or one who has been involved in lengthy litigation before, will always seek a solution without going this far. The novice, on the other hand, gets mad and refuses to back down.

managing the business
get legal: protect yourself from risk

Common causes of litigation include:

- dissatisfied customers refusing to pay their bill
- suppliers chasing you for money when you're not happy with what they've delivered
- tenant/landlord disputes, particularly about repairs and making good at the end of a lease
- personal injury claims by people using 'no win, no fee' lawyers.

Some less common causes of litigation are when:

- you're accused of infringing someone's patent
- you've unwittingly infringed a trademark
- local protestors are trying to stop you expanding/building/ selling.

How litigation happens

Litigation can best be described as 'creative writing'. The two parties in the dispute (plaintiff who sues and defendant who is sued) hire solicitors. The solicitors then write to each other on behalf of their respective clients.

To the layperson (you and me!) this correspondence always seems to:

- exaggerate the claim
- assume that the plaintiff is right in every respect
- make very bold claims and counterclaims
- be written in language that makes it all seem very alarming.

top tip

Litigators describe situations and eventualities in terms that are meant to be frightening. Always read solicitors' letters objectively and never respond immediately. Always take time to calm down and reflect before replying.

Here are some sensible rules of thumb to bear in mind.

- **Small plaintiff, big defendant**: this means it could be long, bloody and so expensive that even winning might feel like losing. It might be cheaper to accept that the big guy is going to 'kick sand in your face' and move out of his patch.

- **Big plaintiff, small defendant**: it might be cheaper to find a quick and painless solution as big plaintiffs rarely stop chasing. If your solicitor wants to keep fighting ask him or her to share some of the financial risk!

Alternatives to litigation

Rather than go in with your solicitor 'guns blazing', try some less aggressive approaches first. Here are some you can consider.

- **Reflect**: is this really a dispute or am I simply being pig-headed? Worse, am I actually in the wrong but unwilling to admit it? Sometimes an apology is the best way out.

- **Discuss**: all disputes are best settled by having a calm conversation with the other party. When doing this, always give your opponent opportunities to back down without losing face. Pride is a powerful motivator in litigation.

- **Compromise**: when you're arguing about money this is easy. You can work out the difference between the sum you each think is fair, then agree to halve it, pay it and move on. When negotiating a compromise, always make sure both sides come out with something positive.

- **Arbitrate**: solicitors and other professionals can do this on your behalf. It takes out the emotion and avoids courtroom confrontation.

top tip

The best way to avoid litigation is to avoid doing things likely to provoke it. Clear communication with your customers and your own strong brand can help you avoid time-consuming conflict.

managing the business
get legal: protect yourself from risk

Intellectual property made simple

If you're starting a new business to capitalise on your new invention you will want to protect every aspect of it from emulation. If you're an experienced inventor you'll know that, unless your invention is a sure-fire winner, protection is probably going to be a waste of money.

Intellectual property is both simple and complex. Simple in that the various kinds of protection are easy enough to explain and

intellectual property is both simple and complex

understand. Complex in that, even when you have everything covered, if a huge corporation decides to copy your idea you probably can't afford the legal costs and risk involved with fighting them off. That said, you don't have to look far to find examples of where David the inventor has managed to slay Goliath the plagiarising corporate giant.

top tip

To protect an invention with a patent you must not have shown it to anyone first. Talk to a patent attorney before you talk to anyone else.

Types of intellectual property

What you are doing is asserting and proving your right to something you have created. Here are some different things you can do.

Copyright

If you have produced words, music, images or drawings that are original work they are automatically protected by copyright. You don't have to do anything, although it makes sense to assert your copyright by marking copies with the symbol ©.

Trademarks

Trademarks are just that – logos and other visual representations of your business or brand. You can register them to create a 'registered mark', denoted by ®, or simply stake your claim by adding ™ as a suffix to the trademark.

Patents

These protect new inventions and cover how they work, what they do, how they do it, what they are made of and how they are made. You have to register a patent.

Designs

Designs can be protected too. They apply to products that have a distinctive shape, look, colour or texture.

Sharing your secret

The experienced entrepreneur or inventor knows that without a market an invention has little value. The Patent Register is packed with good ideas that will never, ever be turned into products.

The dilemma facing the new inventor is this: how do I keep the idea secret and check out if it has market potential? Research, common sense and instinct can help. So can a 'Non Disclosure Agreement' (NDA).

If your prospective customer or collaborator signs an NDA first you can still patent the idea. The NDA prevents those who sign it from divulging the trade secrets you then reveal to them.

You can download draft NDAs from the internet. Many patent attorneys offer them on their websites. It is in their interest for you not to jeopardise your chances of protecting your intellectual property.

How to obtain patents and registered trademarks

Inventors often prefer inventing things to manufacturing and marketing them. They know that their invention or idea has greater value if it is protected. Registering your intellectual property proves to a potential buyer that:

- someone has checked to see if the idea is unique or actually already patented by someone else

- the vital elements of the idea are safe from being copied
- they can sue anyone who copies the idea.

The process is complicated and lengthy. You need to choose a patent agent or trademark attorney to help you. No experienced entrepreneur attempts to do this on their own.

top tip

An 'expensive' intellectual property specialist can cost you less than a 'cheap' one. They often need to do less work for you than you might think.

and finally...

Now think about:

- What would happen if illness prevented you from working?
- What are the risks that your business faces?
- What intellectual property do you have and how is it protected?

get a team
shortcuts to recruitment and staff management

- ☑ Employees or temps – making the choice
- ☑ Defining roles
- ☑ Measuring performance

Why you need people

However much you are on your own, your ability to make money is limited by the time and energy you can put into your business. Once you start to delegate to others, your opportunities are far less limited. All you need to do is motivate others to do the work for less pay than they are earning you.

> the move from one-man band to the first employee is a huge, terrifying leap

For many entrepreneurs, the move from one-man band to the first employee is a huge, terrifying leap. It really is one of the biggest barriers the entrepreneur has to cross in search of success.

Why some people sub-contract and others hire staff

There are several options to consider when deciding whether to sub-contract or hire staff. Each has its merits and drawbacks. Much depends on your long-term aspiration. If you are planning steady growth, then hiring staff might be the best option. If you're expecting peaks and troughs of demand, then perhaps you need to consider another option.

Here are some ways to get things done.

Recruiting employees

Employees are people you hire, train, motivate and have a long-term commitment to retain.

Good points:

- motivated employees can move mountains to get things done
- you build and benefit from your own reservoir of knowledge and expertise.

Bad points:

- employees become an overhead cost so there's less flexibility
- you need to recruit carefully as mistakes are hard to rectify.

Agency staff

These are people employed by a staff agency that you can hire by the hour, day, week or month.

Good points:

- manpower when you need it and not when you don't
- labour costs linked to activity (a variable cost).

Bad points:

- no guarantees you get the same people every time
- agency staff cost more per hour than employees.

Sub-contractors

These are specialist businesses that do things on your behalf.

Good points:

- you can negotiate a deal that suits you both
- prices are agreed so you get no surprises if things go wrong.

Bad points:

- you have less control over quality
- you can become overly dependent on your sub-contractors (tail wagging dog).

top tip

If you are good at what you do, but not so good at selling, then being a sub-contractor to others might be a good business model for you.

Training temps makes sense

John set up a business to manufacture machines for a large corporate client. This one client represented almost his company's entire turnover. He wanted to tailor his costs to the flow of orders, so that he could meet peaks of demand without having workers standing idle when there were no orders.

He rented a factory unit and fitted it out in a way that made product assembly logical and simple. Everything was colour-coded and each work station had diagrams illustrating what had to be done there.

He then worked with a staff agency that provided workers when he needed them. He paid a little over the going rate and made sure everyone was happy at work. He even bought takeaway meals for those who volunteered to work late when an urgent order had to be completed.

As the business grew and more customers were won, he found it made sense to recruit some full-time staff. Not surprisingly, he recruited some of the best people the agency had placed with him as temps over the previous months.

Temp to perm

This is a common phrase in the employment agency world. You have someone on a temporary basis from an agency and then decide you'd like to offer them a full-time job. The agency then charges you a fee for the transfer. It's a good way to hire staff as you get to try before you buy.

Things to do before you recruit

Recruiting your first employee is a huge step for the new entrepreneur. You find yourself sharing the business tasks and challenges with someone who sees your enterprise in a very different way from you. They've got a job; you've got a business. You're realising a vision; they're working to pay the bills.

Being an employer for the first time can be a difficult time. You can feel both frustration and responsibility. They won't be as enthusiastic as you but they will expect a lot from you. Getting it right from the outset is one of the new entrepreneur's biggest challenges.

The experienced employer has learned how to deal with the practicalities of employing people. We can learn a lot from their experience.

What's the job?

The smaller the organisation, the harder it is to define the job. In a large organisation there are structures and clearly-defined roles. There are pay scales, role hierarchies and established practices and procedures. In a very small organisation these distinctions have to be created.

the smaller the organisation, the harder it is to define the job

The business starter usually starts off working alone, doing whatever needs to be done. But the first employee will expect a clearly-defined set of responsibilities.

To define what the job consists of you need to consider:

- which tasks can most easily be done by someone else
- whether this is a long-term or a short-term need

- what skills the job requires

- how you will measure performance

- if your business continues to grow, what you would like this person to be doing in two years' time.

It's better to hire people to do the things you can't do well yourself than to hire people to do what you can do well yourself.

Then you need to write a job specification that defines:

- what the person will be expected to do

- who they will report to

- where they will work

- when they will work and how flexible the hours will be

- what the pay and other terms of employment will be.

Benchmarking

Benchmarking is a big word with a very simple meaning. In the context of planning to employ someone, it simply means checking to see what other employers are offering. The savvy entrepreneur does this by:

- reading job ads to see how other people describe similar roles

- downloading job application packs to get detailed information about how others have defined the job

- checking with trade associations to find comparative pay levels, etc.

- asking people he or she knows to share their information/ experience.

There is little point in re-inventing the wheel. You're far better basing your job specification on what others have done before.

managing the business
get a team: shortcuts to recruitment and staff management

Benchmarking in practice

Gerald and Lucy opened a small classical music shop in their home city. Both were classical music buffs. Gerald also played piano and Lucy the flute. The shop soon became a success, meeting the needs of customers not provided for by the major retailers whose focus was on more popular music.

Then Lucy became pregnant. The couple were delighted, but needed to hire a member of staff. They worked out what they needed then rang a few people they knew who had similar shops in other cities. One even sent over a job specification they'd used and another the words they'd used in a recruitment ad. This saved the couple a lot of work and gave them confidence that they'd got everything covered.

Why people use recruitment agencies

At first glance, recruitment agencies are an expensive option. They typically charge a significant percentage of the first year's salary for the people they recruit. Advertising and any psychometric profiling can cost extra.

When you're a very small business hiring people, paying these fees, as well as paying the person you hire, can seem daunting. It also has to be said that recruitment agencies can be very pushy. Even if you've advertised a job, they can bombard you with offers of 'the perfect candidate'. This aggressive approach can heighten your concern that they're trying to rip you off.

What it costs to recruit on your own

It's easy to underestimate the true cost of recruiting on your own. You will tend to overlook the value of your own time. Hours spent recruiting are not hours spent making money!

The greatest potential cost to your business, however, is finding out too late that you've hired the wrong person. New recruits may not work out for many reasons. The negative impact on your business is always the same: disruption, stress and more expense.

Try working out what each of the following activities could really cost you:

- defining the job specification
- making sure the job fits with the norm for that role
- preparing and placing a recruitment ad
- sifting through applications and creating a shortlist
- writing to those not shortlisted
- arranging interviews
- interviewing
- taking up references.

Calculate how much time this will really take you and work out a budget. It will probably surprise you. Now work out how you'll find the time; that's even harder. If you weren't already stretched you wouldn't be recruiting, would you?

Choosing an agency

It's obvious when you think it through. The best way to find the right agency is to put yourself in the shoes of the person you want to recruit. You don't know them yet but you can guess where they might be looking for a job. They'll either be actively seeking a new challenge or have listed themselves with an agency as being interested.

All agencies have specialisms. You'll spot these when you check them out. Depending on the job, you might choose an agency that is:

- local and covers a wide range of jobs
- national and specialises in the skills you're seeking
- fits somewhere in between.

Experienced agency users will always:

- try to negotiate the fees down, or have more service included for the money
- take lightly the claim that 'we have the perfect person for you on our books'

- stick to the rules and try not to bypass the agency once someone suitable is hired.

Headhunting staff

Poaching staff from someone else can seem tempting. Some agencies specialise in this. It's called 'search', rather than 'selection' which is the usual process of advertising and shortlisting.

headhunting works best for very senior positions

You may have been approached by a headhunter yourself at some time. It's a very flattering experience. You also probably know of people employed by rivals that you'd like to have in your team.

Headhunting works best for very senior positions. It works less well in the small business sector. Those experienced in recruitment know that headhunting can lead to disappointment, because the person you headhunt:

- uses your offer to improve their deal where they are
- turns out to be too steeped in the industry to offer much that's new
- tries to make your firm work the same way as the one they've left
- says they'll bring loyal customers, who, when it comes to the crunch, stay with their original supplier.

top tip

When recruiting you always get what you pay for. Good people command a premium and are usually worth the extra investment.

Quick ways to measure staff performance

There are three good reasons why the seasoned entrepreneur measures performance. They are:

1 To monitor efficiency.

2 To identify problems.

3 To motivate people.

Monitoring efficiency

When you buy a car, you have an expectation that it will perform in a certain way. Warning lights will let you know if it runs too hot or gets low on fuel or oil. It might also have an onboard computer to calculate fuel economy and might also alert you when it needs servicing.

Quick ways to monitor efficiency include:

- a clear job description that states what the person does
- personal objectives that are regularly reviewed and agreed
- simple processes and systems that enable both worker and manager to measure how well things are going.

top tip

Remember that, in most cases, the quality of work is as important as the quantity. Measure efficiency in terms of 'better' not just 'more'.

Identifying problems

You want to know as early as possible when things are going wrong. You also want to discover knowledge and skill gaps that need to be filled. People often don't know what they don't know. You have to help them find that out.

Problems that good performance measurement can highlight include:

- skill gaps, because output differs from industry norms
- attitude gaps, because people don't see the relevance or significance of what they're being asked to do
- component/ingredient/supplier problems, because things are not going according to plan.

Motivating people

Measurement of performance enables everyone to know how well things are going. Staff motivation is important if you want everyone to share your enthusiasm.

Quick ways to motivate include:

- offering incentives to meet production targets
- shareing the additional profit from 'add-on' sales
- making it easy for your people to see how they can influence success.

Also remember to agree annual overarching goals for each employee and review these in an annual appraisal. This should be a two-way exchange.

Maverick entrepreneur

Ricardo Semler wrote Maverick, *a book that describes how he transformed his father's manufacturing business. He shared the targets and challenges and let his people work in teams to decide how they were going to achieve success. In time his people came to decide their own working hours, pay and bonuses. He simply created an environment where each of his employees felt able to benefit from delivering the results the company wanted from them. It can take a lifetime to become confident enough to delegate to and motivate people in the way that Semler did.*

Also read The Seven Day Weekend, *a sequel to* Maverick *which describes how Semler's management technique evolved over time.*

and finally...

Now think about:

- What do you now need to delegate to others?
- How can you best match labour need to work demand?
- In what ways will you measure performance simply?

get a life
shortcuts to work/life balance

- ☑ Manage your time
- ☑ Manage your stress
- ☑ Get the right balance in your life

How to say no

Successful people always seem busy. But busy does not mean having too much to do, it means making time for the things you want to do.

The biggest difference between the new entrepreneur and the old hand is this: the experienced entrepreneur has learned how to say no. When you start a business you say yes to whatever comes along. When you become successful you find yourself

> **the experienced entrepreneur has learned how to say no**

confronted by too many opportunities. You have to say no. Saying no to somebody:

- ☑ can win you their respect, particularly if you introduce an alternative
- ☑ makes people value you more when you do say yes
- ☑ shows that you are focused and selective.

top tip

If you're not busy but want to appear to be, make it clear that you're making an exception to help the other person, not yourself. Say something like: 'I don't usually take these on, but I am impressed by what you're trying to do and, just this once, will find a way to fit you in.'

Managing your time

There has been much written about time management. You can attend courses, hire someone to help you de-clutter your life, or you can shortcut all that and follow these few very simple rules.

- Focus: know what you want to do and only accept opportunities that take you closer to your personal ambition.
- Prioritise: categorise tasks so that the most important can take priority over the less important. There are only three categories of task:
  - critical – things you must do before all others
  - important – things you need to do that have deadlines
  - interesting – things you do when tired or want to be distracted.
- Be realistic: don't try to fit too much into the day. Better to complete one task properly than to bodge two.
- Avoid distraction: put the phone on voicemail and turn off your email for part of each day. Use that time to work on critical projects.
- Meetings: before agreeing to any meeting think hard about whether you really do need to be there. Avoid persuading yourself that you need to be there – to represent the organisation, to be seen, in case you miss anything. Only go to meetings you have to attend and be prepared to leave early if there's nothing more you can contribute.

■ Don't procrastinate: the cluttered desk has almost become a visual metaphor that depicts the busy person. The opposite is true. People without enough to do fill their desk with 'stuff' so they can look busy and important. Your first reaction to anything new that comes your way is probably right. Whenever anything new comes your way, decide straight away whether it's to be done, delegated or dumped.

Why leisure time is vital

It's too easy to think that work is more important than play. In reality, both are important. You need to give leisure pursuits equal ranking to work activities. It's fine to:

■ treat your gym sessions as firm bookings in your diary that can't be moved for work commitments

■ say no to an evening engagement because you've planned a night in with your partner

■ build time into your schedule to visit somewhere interesting when travelling on business.

Leisure activity enhances business performance

Richard's company sells specialist software used by charities. He tends to do the selling and has three people in the office who provide client support and back up. He spends a couple of days a week on the road.

His passion outside work is architecture and he loves visiting old churches. He builds enough time into his travel schedule to visit an old building close to each of his sales calls. This gives him an hour to relax and reflect before he makes a client visit. This enables him to negotiate more effectively. It also means that if his train is delayed, he is not late for his meetings.

managing the business
get a life: shortcuts to work/life balance

14

Fast ways to manage your stress

We all respond differently to stress. Some people seem able to take huge personal risks without showing any signs of worry. Others are so easily daunted they keep their heads down and never take a risk at all.

You need to understand quickly how you deal with stress. The process of becoming successful almost inevitably demands that you visit the extremities of your comfort zone and at times leave it altogether.

What is stress?

Stress is an instinctive human response to danger. Once it gave us the alertness and adrenaline to flee from physical danger. Today we rarely need to run away so we don't resolve the stress through intense physical activity. That's one reason why stress can be so damaging.

stress is an instinctive human response to danger

Stress can be caused by the following factors.

- Danger: an unexpected threat, for example a masked gunman rushes into your shop.

- You: things are worrying you. These might even be things you can't change, such as an embarrassing recent event.

- Your surroundings: noise, overcrowding, heat or cold. Imagine being trapped in a lift full of complete strangers for an hour.

- Tiredness: we are all only human. We get tired. Fatigue lowers our resistance to anything that might stress us.

Symptoms of stress

Stress affects the way we perform. Our judgement can be affected, we can become irrational and eventually seriously ill. As well as spotting signs of stress in yourself, it's important as your enterprise grows to spot it in those you employ. Symptoms of stress can include:

- physical problems such as frequent headaches, increased wind and trips to the toilet; impotence can also be a sign of stress

- emotional problems such as feelings of paranoia, irrational fear and a growing sense of gloom that overlays every aspect of life

- Self medication, for example increased consumption of caffeine, tobacco and alcohol. Comfort eating can also become more than a habit.

How to cope

We all need some stress, but the savvy entrepreneur knows how to manage the levels of stress in him/herself and those within the team. Here are some secrets of successful stress management:

- manage workload so that you can feel busy, but not overwhelmed

- manage expectations so that you don't promise what's impossible to deliver

- manage time for exercise, as physical fitness builds your stress resistance

- manage to share, with a trusted partner, colleague or mentor, rather than keep your worries to yourself.

When stress is unavoidable

There are times when stress is unavoidable – a peak workload, an unexpected problem or a personal crisis of some kind. What matters is how you handle the stress and particularly how you pass it on to those you employ.

Employees can too often have their boss's stress 'dumped' on them. Emotional outbursts and phrases such as 'It's all your fault' or 'You caused the problem, you sort it out' are not helpful.

When managing a stressful situation:

- define exactly what the issue is and what needs to be done

- lead assertively, positively and unemotionally

- avoid subjective criticism – 'what' is more important than 'how'

managing the business
get a life: shortcuts to work/life balance

14

- create space by diverting or delaying other activities
- listen carefully to feedback, concerns and suggestions.

Why balance is important

Holidays are important and so is making time for yourself during the working week. The example of Richard, earlier in this chapter, shows that arriving in a new town an hour or two ahead of an important meeting has two benefits. Firstly it gives you time to relax and prepare in your mind for the meeting; secondly it makes the journey less stressful as you have time in hand.

Time off is important for all kinds of reasons. Here are some of them.

Family is important

Our family, parents, partner, children and siblings have an important role to play in our emotional wellbeing. Most people will say that they work to 'provide for their family'. In the case of the entrepreneur, this powerful motivating driver is often very strong. The entrepreneur often wants to give his or her children a better start in life than they had themselves.

Making time for family is, as we all know, as important as providing for them financially. Finding that time can be quite a challenge. Successful entrepreneurs often:

- set aside time every week for a family activity and resist the temptation to work on that day – they make time off a habit
- realise that a couple of hours off for a specific treat can be more useful than a whole day together doing not much at all
- combine work with a holiday – for example, visiting another country can provide opportunities to see how businesses like yours operate there.

Time to think

Think of your brain as an engine. When you're working flat out it's under load and so unable to rev freely. Take your brain out of gear and it can race. That's the time when new ideas emerge.

The busy entrepreneur knows that even small breaks in the routine can create opportunities for reflection and creative thinking. These can include:

> **even small breaks in the routine can create opportunities for reflection and creative thinking**

- ◪ taking your coffee break away from your desk and its distractions

- ◪ making time for a lunch break and perhaps a walk in a local park

- ◪ investing in a First Class ticket on the train so that you travel in a more relaxed environment

- ◪ setting aside a few half days a year to go somewhere quiet for a good think

- ◪ visiting art galleries where you see images that encourage you to see life differently.

top tip

Some successful people turn off their mobile phones and Blackberries™ when travelling. Being free from interruption lets you think more clearly.

Going on retreat

Robert runs a marketing business. Every summer he takes a week off and travels on his own to a remote island off the Northumbrian coast. He takes with him walking boots and waterproofs so he can spend the whole week outdoors. Each day on his retreat he considers one aspect of his life. He reviews what he likes and what he wants to change. He writes down the things he wants to do differently when he goes home.

As the years have gone by the task has become easier. This is because he always takes his notes from earlier years with him. He is able to recognise what has been achieved as he sets about planning the coming twelve months.

Initially Robert went on these solitary retreats to manage his stress. Over five years he used them to totally transform his life and business.

managing the business
get a life: shortcuts to work/life balance

14

How to help a workaholic

The work ethic that drives many of us to work long hours also

**the workaholic finds
it difficult to cut down**

drives most entrepreneurs. It's fair to say that without hard work, few businesses succeed. It's also fair to say that managing growth is one of the biggest challenges facing the entrepreneur. If business growth is too:

- slow, opportunities can be lost and rivals can overtake you
- fast, you can be exposed to unnecessary risk and perhaps run out of money.

There is nothing wrong with letting a business grow at what feels like the right pace. If this means you don't have to work very hard then actually that's OK. No one is going to tell you off.

Being driven

In common with any other addict, the workaholic finds it difficult to cut down. Even if the business doesn't need them for 80 hours a week they still put in the hours. The problem when you overwork is that you:

- become less productive or more inefficient – so you feel compelled to work harder to compensate
- neglect your family and social life – so you don't see work in its true context
- develop distorted concepts of what's important and what's not.

When you're on that treadmill, going ever faster and faster, you lose the ability to see that you have a problem. That's why it's important that when any of us sees someone in this situation, we gently point it out.

Cutting back

Easing off the throttle and learning to coast occasionally is tough for the workaholic. If it's you, your business partner or someone you employ, you need to develop a strategy to help that individual to cut back.

Techniques successful people use to cut back include the following.

- Improved time management – delegating, prioritising tasks and pacing yourself by not over-committing.

- Gradually cutting down your hours – perhaps aiming to get home an hour earlier. This forces you to delegate or dump work as you have less time to do it in.

- Make fun as important as work – book yourself sessions at the gym and give these equal importance to business meetings. Do the same with social engagements.

- Get to know the people you work with – or more specifically, use coffee and lunch breaks to find out about the people you work with or employ. It's amazing how useful it can sometimes be to know what additional interests and skills people have.

top tip

When scheduling your time, don't just put appointments in your diary. Put in project work time as well. This reduces the temptation to fill your time with meetings, leaving too little time to actually do any work.

Workaholics anonymous

You won't be surprised to learn that there really is an organisation called 'Workaholics Anonymous' (www.workaholics-anonymous.org). It's based in California. Their website states that, 'Our primary purpose is to live without compulsive work, worry, or anxiety, one day at a time, and to help other workaholics to recover.'

and finally...

Now think about:

- How much of your work time do you currently waste?

- When was the last time you took time off and how inspired were you?

- Which people do you know who might need your help to ease back?

managing the business
get a life: shortcuts to work/life balance

14

buying better
shortcuts to getting the best deals from suppliers

- ☑ Why it's crucial to be a good buyer
- ☑ How to buy better
- ☑ Partnerships – making your money go even further

Putting buying in context

You only have to look at how supermarkets in the UK dominate the food sector to realise that big buyers can really set the terms by which they buy. They demand exacting quality standards and are strict about how you transport to their depots, as well as telling you what they're going to pay and when.

The corner shop on the other hand has no sway with its wholesaler. It buys what the cash and carry stocks at the price they choose to sell it at. Then the shop tries to sell the goods at a profit.

Why buying is as important as selling

Every successful entrepreneur will tell you that buying well is even more important than selling well. The lower you can keep your costs the greater scope you have to offer competitive prices. Or on the other hand you can maintain your prices and make more profit.

Profit vs turnover

There is an old adage: 'turnover is vanity; profit is sanity'. The experienced entrepreneur will have developed beyond the point where they are impressed by hitting bold sales targets at the expense of margin.

Let's look at an example of two businesses – Budget Beds and Ace Beds. Which of the two would you prefer to own?

Company	Budget Beds	Ace Beds
Annual sales – units	1,000	1,000
Annual sales	£200,000	£180,000
Annual purchases	£120,000	£90,000
Overhead costs	£50,000	£50,000
Annual profit	£30,000	£40,000

Both have the same number of customers and the same overhead costs. Their workloads are equal, but Ace Beds makes more money as well as selling cheaper beds. To the customer, Ace represents the best deal. And because Ace and its customers pay less for their beds, it also makes more profit. Alternatively, Ace could sell fewer beds and still make the same profit. It is better able to survive a downturn in sales.

It also has to be said that it's easier to negotiate a discount with one supplier for 1,000 beds than to charge a premium price to the 1,000 customers over the year who buy a bed.

Managing your overheads

It's good practice to take time out to review all of your overhead costs at least once a year. This is true of every business, even the self-employed tradesperson who only needs to buy a few tools.

For example, a window cleaner checking their annual costs discovers that it's possible to:

- reduce the insurance bill for their van by £100 per year
- buy diesel at a supermarket and save £150 per year
- change mobile phone tariffs and save £50 per year.

> review all of your overhead costs at least once a year

The total savings of £300 don't look like much at first. However, they represent the income from six jobs that would normally take three days to do. Even in this example, the savings are worth making.

How good buyers get the best deals

The skills you need to be good at selling also stand you in good stead when you're buying. The process is almost identical. In fact practising buying helps your sales technique because it gives you an insight into how your customers might be feeling when you're selling to them.

Here are the things all good buyers have in common.

Have alternatives

There's no such thing as a single source supplier. There's always somewhere else you can buy what you need. If you don't have an alternative supplier, find one and build a relationship. No one can afford to be reliant on one single source of products or raw materials.

In some sectors, for example franchising, you are restricted by the franchisor and have no choice. Everywhere else it's vital to have alternatives. When you're buying, your supplier has to know you have the ability to walk away from the deal. That gets you the best deal.

Hold back from saying yes

Good buying practice is about squeezing concessions out of your supplier before say yes to buying. Once they know you're going to buy it's harder to improve the deal. Post commitment, you will both work on the details and fine tune arrangements to suit both parties. The skilled negotiator will go for as much as possible before committing anything.

Ask for the impossible

You know the old saying, 'if you don't ask, you don't get'. This is very appropriate to the experienced buyer. We soon become used to buying advertising at prices well below the journal's published rate card. We too often forget to try for discounts when buying things for our business.

ask for much more than you think you'll get

Although clearly you need to be reasonable in what you ask for, you should still ask for much more than you think you'll get. Remember this is not just about price. For example:

- ask for the current price to be held for 12 months so you know you can maintain your pricing level too
- ask for free delivery, or free storage, and 'just in time' delivery
- ask for relevant training for your staff to be provided
- ask for marketing and after-sales support.

Give to gain

The inexpert buyer expects the supplier to make a series of concessions. This won't happen unless you give a little as well. Good buyers trade concessions. You will both be trying to concede things that cost you less but are worth much more to the other person. For example:

- if the supplier has a large warehouse and you have no storage, 'just in time' despatch will be very useful to you and of little consequence to the supplier
- if your supplier's truck passes your gate on the way to another customer, giving you free delivery will cost them nothing. You in turn agree to hold stock and allow the supplier to top up when passing.

Remember that buying, as in any negotiation, is about seeking out the best solution for both parties. The better it is for you both, the longer the trading relationship will last.

buying, as in any negotiation, is about seeking out the best solution for both parties

Whenever you buy anything ask the vendor to confirm that this really is the best deal they can offer. This makes them pause and reflect on what they're selling you. Wait for them to come back and either say yes it is or offer some concession. Often, the longer they think about it the easier it'll be to push them a little harder.

Building partnerships with suppliers

The best deals are often the most creative ones. They blur the traditional boundaries between customer and supplier, enabling both businesses to benefit.

Perfect partnership

Roland has a very successful coffee shop/restaurant in a large city. His outlet competes head-on with major players such as Costa Coffee and Starbucks. He has created a unique and popular meeting place that people choose for its good coffee and friendly service.

The office building next door was refurbished and re-opened as a prestigious training academy for the financial services industry. They wanted a cafeteria and Roland, coincidentally, wanted to grow his business.

He replicated his café in the new building and a door was put in to connect this with his existing outlet. The academy gained a popular in-house café with a ready-made reputation. Roland was able to prepare sandwiches and paninis for both in the same kitchen, making it a very profitable expansion.

Both Roland and the academy benefited. Prices were lower in the academy than in the café next door and Roland was able to increase his turnover without the overheads of opening a second café.

Why partnerships work

In today's business world trading relationships can be deep and complex. Organisations focus on their strengths and when times get tough divest themselves of non-core activities. This corporate single-mindedness creates opportunities.

Examples

- *Managers of marginalised functions sometimes buy out their activity and create a profitable business.*

- *Resources may be shared between organisations. For example, an IT department might support other networks as well as its own.*

- *Suppliers and customers can see opportunities to diversify and do more for each other. For example, a sub-contract metalworking company is also asked to assemble the products they currently make components for.*

Blurring the supplier/customer boundary enables both businesses to do what they do best, reduce their costs and protect themselves from unnecessary risk.

What to look for

Every business relationship is unique to some extent. There is no obvious formula you can apply to identify opportunities for an innovative partnership. However, there are some questions you can ask yourself:

- What aspects of my business give me the greatest angst?
- What's missing? Is it skill, time, space, logistics, etc.?
- How could my supplier help and at what cost?
- What's in it for them?

The key point to remember is that both parties have to benefit from the partnership.

To help you see how perhaps you could build a partnership with your suppliers, giving you real market advantage, here are a few more examples to stimulate your thinking.

Examples

■ *A distributor of grain sampling equipment used at animal feed mills takes over the installation, commissioning and servicing of the equipment they sell. Previously, the supplier had handled these aspects of the sale but this was costly and inflexible. Moving the boundary enables the manufacturer to reduce costs and focus on making things. The distributor not only increases its margin, but also has lower costs so can be more competitive in the marketplace.*

■ *A white goods manufacturer wants to outsource storage and distribution. It has a warehouse on site, but managing this is becoming a distraction. The plan is to outsource everything from the end of the production line to the customer.*

A small logistics company started by a team recently made redundant as part of a corporate reshuffle has the skills and knowledge but lacks the resources. They move their business on to the white goods manufacturer's site and operate from its warehouse. The white goods manufacturer gains because what have formerly been direct costs now become variable costs. Furthermore, because the logistics team stores for other people in the same warehouse, they are able to make a good profit and charge their host very competitive rates.

Fast ways to save money

Spending money is easy. Making it is tougher! That's why the savvy entrepreneur digs out good deals and spends as little as possible. The novice buys new, buys from the obvious place and sometimes buys things he or she simply doesn't need.

There are very few aspects of business where you can't make significant savings. Let's consider some of the most important.

Equipment

Why buy new when you can buy second-hand equipment? People trade up all the time as their businesses grow. You can buy perfectly good second-hand equipment from:

- dealers who accept trade-ins against new machines
- companies that are growing and sell what they have outgrown
- auctions where surplus stock is sold off
- insolvency practitioners realising the asset value of a failed business.

top tip

With pre-owned equipment there's always the fear that running costs will be high. Arrange a maintenance contract so that you know exactly what your running costs will be.

Premises

It's good to have your own business premises with your own front door. Most businesses start in serviced offices or at home so it's natural to want something a little more swanky as soon as you can afford it.

Here are some points you might not always think to consider.

- Location – unless you're a retailer, you may be better to opt for a better place in a less desirable location. If you don't get customers visiting you, do you really need your own ground floor entrance?
- Short leases are often available in office buildings; perfect if you're not sure what you'll need in a year's time. A short lease can get you a smart address at a knock-down rent at the time your business may need both.
- Sharing with someone else can make sense. Students do it at university so why not do the same with your business?

Vehicles

There's a lot of emotion behind the decision to buy a car, van or truck. Being objective can save you a load of cash. Think about:

- buying a less well-known brand of vehicle that comes with a full maintenance package

- buying 'nearly new', not new – many dealers register vehicles to hit sales targets at certain times of year and they then sell them as 'used' at what can be a significant discount

- borrowing a vehicle – sometimes one of your suppliers might let you use one of their vehicles if they can see a clear benefit to them

- hiring when needed – this can sometimes cost less than buying and gives you greater flexibility.

Raw materials

For some businesses the price you pay for the materials you use makes a huge difference to your profitability. If you can buy better you can automatically increase your profits. Those in the know reduce their raw material costs in a number of ways.

- Shopping around. This sounds obvious, but too many people buy from their local supplier rather than going further afield for a better deal.

- Joining a buying group and enjoying collective bulk discounts. Farmers have always done this and many farm buying groups are opening their doors to other types of business too.

- Looking for alternative materials that can reduce the overall cost of production. For example, it can often be cheaper to buy pre-worked components from a specialist sub-contractor than make everything yourself from scratch.

- Reading your trade press and following up on stories about innovations that might help you. If you can't approach the featured company give the journalist who wrote the piece a call.

Finally, the most important thing to remember is that there is nearly always an alternative. Don't let anyone persuade you that they are the only supplier you can use. If you keep your eyes and ears open, you will almost always spot the opportunities that others fail to notice.

managing the business
buying better: shortcuts to getting the best deals from suppliers

and finally...

Now think about:

- ◩ When was the last time you checked that your suppliers were giving you the best deal?

- ◩ How well do you negotiate when buying?

- ◩ Who might you share with to reduce your overhead costs?

16 surviving a downturn
shortcuts to coping with recession

☑ What is a recession?

☑ How can I protect myself?

☑ What do I do if it starts to bite?

Why recessions kill businesses

All economies work in a cycle. Good times are inevitably followed by a downturn from which, in time, things recover. The experienced entrepreneur has seen it all before and knows how to prepare. Those who have recently started their business don't know what to expect. They are the most vulnerable.

Warning signs the inexperienced might not notice

The economists usually describe an economy as being in recession when there have been two successive quarters (periods of three months) of negative growth. That means that overall, output is shrinking.

To put this into context, you need to understand that:

- some businesses actually do better in a recession
- some businesses suffer in a downturn more than others
- economic forecasters don't always get it right.

Who suffers first in a recession?

It's usually the consumer, you and me, that feels the pinch first. Rising interest rates, or increases in prices of staple purchases such as food or fuel, mean the consumer has less free cash to spend. Add to this fears about job security, and in the UK, falling property prices, and everyone keeps their purse in their pocket.

It's usually the consumer that feels the pinch first

Sobering fact: If the 60 million people who live in Britain all spend £20 less a week, that's an awful lot of money not going over the shop counter!

In the business-to-business world a downturn usually sees spending reduced first on:

- marketing – as there are reckoned to be fewer customers to win
- training – as it's considered that improving skills can wait
- capital investment – because people make stuff last a little longer
- construction – because market values will be depressed.

If you're in these sectors, you need to make sure your business is resilient enough to weather the storm.

Who sometimes does well in a recession?

When times are tough price becomes the overriding consideration. So too, paradoxically, does luxury. Businesses seek cheaper suppliers as their own margins get squeezed, so it can be boom time for budget products and services. And the wealthy keep spending in part to insulate them from recession and in part because they have no cause to stop.

In a recession it's the mid-market products and services that suffer. If that's where your business is, you need to think about going up-market.

in a recession it's the mid-market products and services that suffer

What to watch out for

Setting aside the media comment and speculation that inevitably precedes a downturn there are a number of things to look out for. Get into the habit of checking these things regularly and you will have more time to prepare. You will know when a downturn is beginning to affect your business from the following signs.

- More enquiries – as people usually supplied by your rivals shop around. They might be looking for a better deal or, worse, at their credit limit with your rival and wanting to run up a bill with you.

- Fewer enquiries – as potential customers decide to delay purchase.

- Slow payers – as your customers use your money to fund their own cash flow.

- Downgrades – as people strip out the extras they can no longer afford.

- Your own bank – it might well want to talk about reducing your borrowings. Banks always become more cautious.

- On the high street – every shop seems to be having yet another sale.

In time, you will develop an almost instinctive feel for when tough times are heading your way.

How to prepare your plan B

Everyone should have a 'plan B'. This applies as much at home as it does in your business. In fact if your home financial situation means that you can afford to take less income from your business in the tough times you will have a lot more flexibility to cope with recession.

managing the business
surviving a downturn: shortcuts to coping with recession

16

The home plan B

It's good to start at home. If your business has been making good money then you may have become less fussy about domestic expenditure. There's a lot of truth in the saying 'easy come, easy go'.

Here are some things to do at home.

- Check that your mortgage is on the best possible terms. If you're a good credit risk you might be able to better your current deal.

- Check your energy costs. You've probably been too busy to check what you've been paying of late and are probably on a higher tariff than people who've changed supplier recently.

- Pre-pay subscriptions. It's going to be important to look after yourself and so rather than cutting out things like gym membership negotiate a discount and pay for the next year up front.

- Examine your outgoings. See what's important and what you can do without. You don't want to become a hermit but you might choose to entertain at home where it'll cost less and might also be more fun.

- Have a financial review. Allow a trusted independent financial adviser to take a look at your investment and debt. Having rainy day money where you can easily reach it is a good idea.

Finally, list the things you'll do without if things get really tough. Put them in order of priority. Then you'll know what to cut first.

The work plan B

Having practised at home you're now better prepared to draw up your business plan B. It's a very similar process, which is why starting at home is such a good idea.

Here are some things to do at work.

- Check that your borrowings are on the best possible terms. If you're a good credit risk you might be able to better your current deal by changing banks. Banks suffer in a downturn too; they want low risk clients like you.

- Check your input costs. It's easy when you're working flat out to become complacent when suppliers increase their prices. Look at all costs and re-negotiate better deals where you can.

- Offer prompt payment if you can afford it and it will get you a decent discount. Alternatively, negotiate late payment if your supplier is big and you're feeling the pinch.

- Do monthly accounts. Things can change very quickly in a downturn and you need to keep your finger on the pulse.

- Stick to what makes money. Ditch the 'nice to do' things and focus on activities that make money.

Cleaning your client list

Juliette has a cleaning company employing three full-time and around fifteen part-time staff. They have a mix of business and domestic clients. New clients have come largely from recommendation. Juliette is able to charge her domestic customers 15 per cent more than business clients and finds they give her less hassle.

When people began to talk of a recession she started to actively seek more domestic work. She was able to drop her least profitable business client, replacing them with four elderly people who can no longer manage their housework.

Juliette knows that older people are more recession proof and profitable than companies.

Why survivors cut their overheads fast

Most businesses that fail in a recession do so because they don't reduce their costs quickly enough. If your sales fall so must your costs. The alternative is insolvency. People who have experienced business failure know how quickly a profitable business can turn into one making huge losses.

Those encountering a recession for the first time often wait too long before acting. There is also a very natural tendency to deny that things are getting rocky. Denial in the face of disaster is an instinctive human response.

Doing redundancies

In most businesses the wage bill is the largest overhead. Regrettably, it is here that in a downturn you usually need to cut deep and fast. People often find it difficult to make jobs redundant and lose people. The harsh reality is, however, that if you don't make necessary staffing cuts, everyone might lose their job.

if you don't make necessary staffing cuts, everyone might lose their job

There are legal processes for making jobs redundant. (It's always the job, not the person that becomes redundant.) Before embarking on a redundancy programme you need to do the following.

- Take legal advice to ensure you comply with employment law. The alternative could be an expensive prosecution in an employment tribunal.

- Consult fully with all of your staff. Even the most hardened employer can be humbled by the creative solutions suggested by a workforce under threat of redundancy. Listen to their ideas.

- Leave the door open. You might want to re-hire the people you're losing at some time in the future.

top tip

The better your people regard you as an employer, the more they'll try to help you when times get tough. It is always a smart move to invest time and energy in being a good boss.

Cutting finance costs

For many businesses, their second largest overhead cost is debt repayment. When your sales fall the cost of servicing the debts incurred as your business grew can be crippling. Here are some potential quick wins.

- Clear out your redundant stock. Over time businesses acquire clutter, unwanted components, equipment, etc. Have a massive clear out, turn scrap into cash and sell everything you no longer need.

- Pay a little later. It's best to do this with their consent, but paying people later will give you more cash to play with. Paying suppliers later is a good way to reduce your overdraft.

- Get paid early. Taking deposits, stage payments and early payment from your customers also reduces the overdraft. It has the added bonus of reducing your liability to bad debt too.

- Consolidate your debts. This works in a business as well as at home. It's usually better to have one large loan, ideally secured against assets, than to have several different finance agreements.

Cutting other overheads

Of course you can reduce your investment in marketing and training, but is this wise? If your rivals are cutting back, you could argue for pushing ahead. It is possible to grow market share in a recession.

Other overheads you might cut include:

- accommodation costs, by moving or renegotiating with your landlord

- telephone costs, by using free 'voice over internet' products such as Skype

- energy costs, by making sure that equipment is maintained and that you're buying energy at the best rates

- transport costs, by whatever means you can – sometimes, for example, it can be cheaper to use a carrier than run your own delivery vans.

managing the business
surviving a downturn: shortcuts to coping with recession

16

How people manage to go bust legally and start again

This is not a recommended way of doing business. However, the less scrupulous might well do it and catch you out. Here's what happens.

- Mr X sets up a limited company, XYZ Ltd, and that business becomes a customer of yours.

- You send goods and invoices and you get paid. Everything's fine.

- Mr X becomes a slow payer and you start to worry.

- You receive a letter from an insolvency practitioner telling you that XYZ Ltd is in 'creditors' voluntary receivership. This means that Mr X has decided he can't pay his bills and has declared the business insolvent.

- After the insolvency practitioner has done his job, it is revealed that the company has no money to pay its creditors. You lose out.

- Then you stumble across a new company WXY Ltd. The name is similar and you spot that the managing director is Mr X. You find that WXY Ltd has purchased the assets (stock, work in progress, etc.) from the insolvent company at a knock-down price.

- You discover that the goods you sold the original company are now being sold on by the new one. You seek legal advice and find you can do nothing to recover your debt from the new company. What Mr X has done might appear dodgy but it is legal.

Ways to avoid being caught out by others' insolvency

There are a number of precautions you can take to avoid getting caught like this.

Be strict on payment terms

A failing company will always pay the people who make the most fuss before paying those who don't chase.

Retention of title

This is a legal term you build into your terms of trade. It means the goods remain yours until paid for. When a company goes bust you can exercise your right to retrieve what's not been paid for and therefore is yours. In practical terms this often means visiting the failed business's premises with a representative from the insolvency practice dealing with the matter. You agree what's covered by the paperwork you both have and clearly label it as yours. At some point you can go in and pick it up.

Garnishee order

If your failed customer has already sold on your unpaid-for consignments you can issue a garnishee order. The courts help you do this. It means that instead of the final customer paying the failed business they are required to pay you. Because in practical terms people hold off paying invoices from failed companies you might need to enforce the order to get paid.

How to avoid going bust yourself

However easy it may look to go bust and start again it's rarely advisable. For one thing your reputation takes a severe knock. For another you probably have guaranteed many of your firm's debts and borrowings. This means you have to pay the debts yourself.

Furthermore, if you trade as a sole trader or in a partnership, should your business fail then so do you. Only limited companies have a legal barrier between the business owner and the business's financial liabilities.

The alternative to going bust is to set up a 'company voluntary agreement' if you're a limited company and an 'insolvency voluntary agreement' if you're not. A specialist accountant will help you do this. It means that your creditors agree to take a proportion of what's owed, usually over a period of time, and write off the rest. They accept this because they've been convinced that it's better to get some money than potentially none at all.

and finally...

Now think about:

- How well prepared are you to survive a recession?

- What are the signs to watch in your business sector?

- When did you last prune out unnecessary costs?

selling your business
shortcuts to making it worth lots

- ◪ Why all businesses should be for sale
- ◪ How to add value to your enterprise
- ◪ Quick ways to find a buyer

Why selling is important

Most entrepreneurs recognise that while a business might give you a good living, the real reward only comes when you sell. In fact the focus on building value into an enterprise, then realising it, is what sets the true entrepreneur apart from those who simply want a nice lifestyle.

This chapter tells you what adds value to a business, how to build it in and, finally, how to get your hands on the cash!

> **the real reward only comes when you sell**

How the professionals value a business

The harsh reality is that a business only has a value when someone is prepared to buy it. You only have to look at what happens when a business goes bust to see how little material value there actually is. Equipment, materials, vehicles and even intellectual property are sold at knock-down prices when a business runs out of steam.

As an entrepreneur your job is to achieve the opposite effect. You want people to see so much potential in your business that they'll pay a premium.

top tip

People buy potential, not property!

How are businesses valued?

Every professional adviser has their own formula to calculate the value of a business. The best person to ask first is your accountant. He or she might not be best qualified to value your business but will almost certainly know someone who can.

As a rule of thumb a business is most commonly valued in terms of a multiple of the profits currently being made. Some will monitor the value of quoted companies to give a ready reckoner guide for the sector you operate in. Typically the multiplier is around twelve, so if your business profits are £30,000 it has a value of 12 × £30,000 = £360,000.

Often as important as the actual profits are the turnover/profit trends. The following table shows likely buyer appeal relating to your current performance.

Performance	Buyer appeal
Fairly young and enjoying exponential sales growth	High potential
Not yet profitable but with intellectual property that's getting rave industry media reviews	High potential/high risk
Sales constant year on year and profits consistently very good	Potentially easy to manage (even grow)
Sales falling, profits good	OK if cheap
Declining profits and now making a loss	Distressed sale – possible turnaround

One business; many values

To further confuse the entrepreneur seeking a buyer, one business will have several values. It all depends who's buying and why. Factors that can influence what someone will pay for a business will include:

- how the business fits within a buyer's portfolio: for example, a motor dealer group buying an additional dealership

- the buyer's lifestyle aspiration: for example, someone retiring early and choosing to buy a seaside guest house

- sector contacts: for example, a senior sales manager, recently made redundant, buying a business in the sector where he already has a good reputation

- a buyer's tax situation: sometimes buying a business at a certain time can reduce the buyer's tax liability – this is to your advantage if you're selling.

Preparing your business for sale

Every business should be for sale. The wise entrepreneur is always open to an approach. Indeed one measure of success is the frequency and seriousness of those approaches.

The true entrepreneur then decides whether now is the time to sell or if it's better to hang on for longer. As the sale price needs to reflect potential, as well as past performance, you don't have to wait until you're on the crest of the wave to sell. You can sell whenever someone makes the right offer.

If it's your first business, you'll feel a strong sense of ownership. That's both natural and important; you've got to live the business in the early stages. However, as you prepare your business to sell you need to make sure everything is in order.

When to sell

The experts say it can take a couple of years to get a business ready for sale. There's a lot to be said for always being ready to sell. All of

managing the business
selling your business: shortcuts to making it worth lots

17

there's a lot to be said for always being ready to sell

the things you need to have in place will do more than make a business more saleable. They'll make it more focused and profitable too. That's why it's good to always be ready.

Keeping it separate

A limited company needs a separate identity, separate banking and annual accounts of its own. A sole trader or partnership is not necessarily so easily divisible from its owner(s). In fact many self-employed people run their business through a personal bank account and work from home.

A good accountant can usually work with this and often the savings in bank charges seem to justify the fiscal confusion. Then there are all the things your business pays for that strictly speaking are not business expenses. We all have them; for example, the haulier who spends lots on his vintage lorry, or the PR person who enjoys photography and spends ten times what is necessary on cameras.

It's always worth the small cost involved in keeping your business separate from your own affairs.

Profits don't just appear on the bottom line

When a business buyer looks at the books they need to see the business as a clearly independent thing. They will understand that the business might be paying you in several ways, depressing profits, but these need to be easy to see.

If you're successful, your accountant (and perhaps your own interests) will help you to reduce your tax liability. Pension contributions, having your partner and maybe even your kids on the payroll and buying what you want, rather than need, are all devices you might use to pay less tax.

The problem is that, if you then try to value your business in terms of multiples of annual profits, you undervalue the enterprise. Buyers know that you will have many ways of rewarding yourself and you need to be up front about these. After all, your buyer will have used many of the same techniques themselves; otherwise they'd probably not be buying your business.

Good people count

The less your business relies on you the easier it will be to sell. For example, a one-man consultancy business has little real value as all that is valuable sits between the owner's ears. On the other hand, a laundrette is much less dependent on the owner for its day-to-day operation. It simply needs someone there to open the door, take the money and make sure everything is working.

> the less your business relies on your the easier it will be to sell

top tip

Many entrepreneurs hire talented ambitious people and nurture their ambition to buy out the business they work for. This is often the best way to sell a small business.

Ways that businesses are sold

Contrary to what many people think, you don't buy a business in the same way you buy a house. The process is in many ways similar but the payment options are more varied.

The process

However you market your business, whether through a business transfer agent, through your accountant or to people you already know, the process you go through is similar, which is roughly as follows:

1 **Prospectus**: this document is the equivalent of an estate agent's particulars. It defines what the business does, its financial performance and potential. It is in many ways similar to a business plan. In fact because it's written to convince others of the value of your business, rather than to reassure yourself, writing it should prompt a lot of self-examination. That's good.

2 **Confidentiality agreement**: this is vital to make sure that the negotiating parties keep the talks secret.

3 **Due diligence**: this is the process by which both buyer and seller check each other out, rather like the searches a house conveyancer conducts. Both parties need to do it because it's important to know that the buyer, as well as the business being bought, is sound.

4 **Contracts**: these are negotiated, written, checked and agreed. The contract defines the terms of the deal. Specialist lawyers usually prepare these contracts. For big businesses they negotiate them too.

top tip

However tempting it may be to cut corners and save professional fees, always take and follow professional advice.

Types of deal

There are infinite ways to structure the deal. Whatever you and your buyer agree, that is legal and bound by a contract, is possible. The type of deal is often dictated as much by the personal aspirations and needs of the seller as by the financial strength of the buyer. Common types of deal include the following.

Cash purchase

This is quite straightforward. Your buyer parts with the money and you part with the shares/assets of the business. You may or may not be expected to work in the business for a handover period. Your advisers will structure the deal to be as tax efficient as possible.

Stage payments

This is a cash sale but with payments spread over a period of time. This can help you with tax and your buyer with funding. Sometimes the amount and timing of each stage payment is linked to a performance milestone being achieved by the business.

Performance related payment

It's worth noting that linking payments to business performance can mean success for both buyer and seller. It gives the seller incentive to stick around and make sure the business performs. It also means the buyer pays less if things don't develop as predicted.

Earn out

This is popular with professional practices as well as with other kinds of business. There's usually an initial payment, just enough to make the seller feel good, then the rest is paid over a period of up to three years, with amounts linked to business performance. Professional practices like this arrangement as it recognises that not all customers will migrate to the buyer. It also means that the purchase price is funded by the business itself. You don't need to go to the bank for a big loan.

you don't need to go to the bank for a big loan

From earn out to ease out

Sarah was senior partner in a firm of accountants. She wanted to retire and her team decided to buy her out. A sum was agreed, payable over three years. Sarah agreed to remain as a consultant for that period, making sure client handovers were successful and that any problems that arose were sorted out. Her share of the business was 60 per cent, and reduced by 20 per cent per year over the three years.

Who might buy your business?

The professional firms that market companies advertise widely and hold lists of potential buyers. However, many businesses are actually bought by people known to the seller. Not surprisingly, if you know the business well, you're more likely to be confident enough in its potential to put in a bid.

Here are some of the common and more unusual people who might buy a business from you.

Employees

Management buyouts are both common and convenient. All parties know each other well and there are few surprises that can emerge and trip up the process. A management team will often invite people with additional skills they need to buy in with them.

Suppliers

If you are a distributor, or in other ways bridge the gap between your suppliers and their end users, they might buy you. There are many benefits to a wholesaler or manufacturer getting closer to their end users. Two obvious benefits are good market intelligence and a greater margin.

Customers

If you're a small specialist business you might find that some customers view your success as critical to their own organisations' wellbeing. They might buy your business to make sure they retain access to its services. Equally, they might want to gain a competitive edge over their own rivals.

Friends

If you're retiring from what is essentially a lifestyle business, younger friends might be interested in taking it over. People often harbour ambitions like this about a friend's enterprise and never actually tell them until asked.

Neighbours

If you or your business own premises don't overlook your neighbours. They might be seeking room to expand. That means your business is worth far more to them than to others. They might even buy it if it's not actually worth anything as a going concern.

Inward investors

These are overseas companies looking to establish a bridgehead in a country. If they work in your sector, buying you out can give them an instant, known shop window into what for them is an overseas market. You can find inward investors by talking to regional development agencies. These have teams focused on attracting inward investment to their region.

Investors

If your business is big enough, you might be advised to float it on the stock-market. There is also AIM in London, a stock-market specifically for smaller companies.

Floating a company is both hugely expensive and potentially hugely rewarding. It is also one of a number of ways you can sell part of your business to attract investment.

Selling part of your business

Many entrepreneurs realise part of the value of their business to free up cash and introduce new investment. You can do this with any sized business, although the smaller it is the greater the impact having to share it will have on your day-to-day life. The benefits of selling part of your business include:

- you get to see some of your wealth and can invest it to secure your family's future

- you retain part of your business so can enjoy future gains if it grows in value

- you have money to invest in starting/acquiring additional businesses – this is how serial entrepreneurs grow their business empires and spread their risk.

and finally...

Now think about:

- ◪ How can you add value into your business and make it appealing to a buyer?

- ◪ When should you consider selling and why?

- ◪ Who might buy a business and what do they want to find?

index

index

index